Copyright © 2015

ISBN 978-0-9834831-6-8

REGENTVILLE
An Australian History Story

Warren Dent

Acknowledgments

Four ladies have helped this work come to completion. Josie Abrahamson and Fai Dawson both offered suggestions on the content, making it more realistic and precise. Christine LePorte edited and simplified expression in many instances, and Maggie Airncliffe created an outstanding index which should make readers' access to events and people much easier.

Thanks go to all of them for their unselfish input, but all interpretations of economic and political events, historical inaccuracies, and judgments on behavior fall strictly on my shoulders.

Author's Note

This book traces the life of one of the great early Australians – Sir John Jamison. The majority of the story takes place in 1800-1850 in a country first settled as recently as 1788. At that time the land belonged to multiple tribes of black-skinned natives. To them, the government officials, militia, convicts, and free settlers were all rude usurpers of their sacred home. With no written language, their thoughts and feelings never realized the exposure, and publicity that those of the white man enjoyed.

Over time, the original colony grew from a penal settlement into a broad-based civilization with its own unique culture. Men like Sir John were instrumental in creating that culture. Sir John's contributions ranged from sharing better agricultural practices with farmers, financing major inland explorations, creating the first bank, opening the first university, securing trial by jury, supporting convicts rights, and creating just laws for the emerging civilized society.

With journalism and infrastructure in a primitive state, it was not a time for accurate record keeping. All historical documentation suffered from the absence of potentially valid and informative indigenous input. This story is based on years of in-depth physical and electronic research. Where detailed facts were not available for certain events, I have tried to fairly represent the spirit of the populace, the place, the laws, and the character of Sir John. May he rest in peace.

Regentville
An Australian History Story

Table of Contents

1. September 1808, Gothenburg, Sweden

The massive ship lurched unevenly and slammed against the old wooden piers with bone-jarring force. For a moment her timbers shuddered before finally surrendering to the new stability offered. The unexpected jolt made Sven's whole frame tremble and he took a step backwards to avoid falling. Another tooth loosened from his blackened gums and he quickly spat it out on the deck. He resisted the urge to use his fingers to count how many teeth still remained. On the captain's shout he staggered to the rail, dragging the heavy coil of rope over his shoulder. With what little strength he had left he hefted the thick mooring line over the rail, thankful to see it land on the edge of the wharf. Two young dockhands picked it up and secured it around one of the huge metal cleats. The planking groaned and the boat's stern gradually shadowed the watery gap to wharf as the taut lines along the port side pulled the giant war machine towards land.

Garth clapped Sven on the shoulder with his huge calloused hand, and asked, "Did ye get it on the first throw?" Garth's left eyeball protruded and his right eye was red from bleeding, his giant frame bent over from swollen legs and unstable joints.

"Yes, we're home, Garth. Thank the Gods. Maybe the doctors onshore can do what the surgeon couldn't and cure this disease for us. Where's Leif?"

"He didn't make it, Sven. Died earlier this morning, wasted away just as the morning sun rose. One more victim. Of the five of us who signed up together it's just you and me left. And we may join the others soon if we don't get help. Come on, my friend. Let's collect our things, pick up our pay, head to the infirmary, and be rid of this vessel. You'll have to be my guide and hold me up at the same time. Good man."

"I don't know, Garth. We've made it, but now that we're here I wonder if survival will be worth it. Look at you and me. We're cripples. We can hardly walk, our skin is patchwork, our eyes and teeth are broken or rotten. Will our wives even be able to look us in the face? Our kids thought we were heroes going off to war. They probably won't even recognize us. All I hope is that the doctors in the hospital can do something for us. Otherwise I'm not even sure about going home."

"I've had similar thoughts, Sven. But we've served our country and made it home. Many of our shipmates' wives will never see their husbands again. Our wives' feelings will never match theirs—at least we're alive. I believe we have to be thankful and hope they will be too when they see us—no matter what we look like. Come on, matey. Best foot forward."

The *Starkotter* had once been the pride of the fleet. Built in 1790, she was one of nine Hemmema warships designed by the naval architect Fredrik Henrik af Chapman. She'd seen a variety of tours in her time but now was a sorry sight. The war with Russia had extracted a heavy toll. Deck timbers were broken or cracked, one mast had been lost, armaments had fallen overboard, and enemy cannon holes just above the waterline required constant maintenance and repair. She had limped into the harbour with her crew feeling almost shame-faced that their magnificent icon was so damaged and forlorn looking. As soon as they'd made contact with the harbour master they'd reefed the few remaining sails that were still intact, and reluctantly permitted a small pilot boat to attach broadside and manage their final passage to the naval wharf.

No one cheered their arrival, which mirrored that of other warships returning. The boats themselves could be repaired. The same could not be said for the majority of the crew members, however. Not unexpectedly, the sailors' clothes were generally tattered and torn. But it was their countenances and physical injuries and broken bodies that dismayed the onlookers. The tough, young, wiry seamen who had embarked on His Majesty's boats, full of vigor, enthusiasm, and fighting spirit, now looked like old men as they alighted. Many were bent over, bloody and heavily bandaged, struggling to walk, their faces distorted by ugly protrusions with grimaces reflecting deep pain. These weren't just consequences of war wounds, but the results and vestiges of disease. Scurvy, the scourge of sailors everywhere, had had greater impact on these seamen than had fights with the enemy. It was Anders, the chief purser, who helped Sven and Garth down the gangplank and steadied them on the wharf as they struggled to find their land legs once again. Anders was one of the least affected. Maybe it was his slight frame or never-say-die attitude. He ate less of the cured and salted meats and dried grains than anyone else on board, although just recently he'd also started to complain of fatigue, rapid breathing, and fever. Those were the signs they all started out with. Seven months at sea looking for the enemy, fighting when found, making repairs to their battered ship while hidden in deep bays behind the islands in coastal archipelagos, adding only fresh fish to the monotonous diet, and experiencing a much colder summer than expected, had taken its toll. Boredom, injuries, and sickness were one thing. Coupled with despair as they watched their sister ships fatally struck and sunk one after the other, morale had become seriously affected. The sailors could hardly raise a cheer when it was decided to retreat and head home.

For some, the port of Gothenburg was home; for most, however, it was on the farms to the northwest and southeast, some close in, some distant. Located on the west coast, in the southwest area of the country, Gothenburg lay at the mouth of the river Göta älv, which fed into an arm of the North Sea, enabling the city to become a major trading centre. The northern end of the gulf stream helped create a mild climate, albeit with plenty of rain. Historically, in the sixteenth and seventeenth centuries, the configuration of Sweden's borders made Gothenburg strategically important as the country's gateway to the west, located close to both Denmark and Norway. Dutch invaders had the skills needed to build in the marshy areas around the city, and the town was originally designed like a Dutch city such as Amsterdam. Street formations, building locations and styles, and common areas were patterned and carefully planned based on experience back home.

Along with the Dutch, the town also was influenced by Scots who came to settle there. It was not until 1652, when the last Dutch politician in the city's council died, that the Swedes acquired political power over Gothenburg. The city grew as an important port due to its location, and the fact that, together with Marstrand, it was the only city on the west coast that was granted the rights to trade with merchants from other countries. In the eighteenth century, fishing was its most important industry, and after the Swedish East India Company was founded in 1731, the city flourished, due to its foreign trade via highly profitable commercial expeditions to Asian countries.

The Navy established a secondary base and became a significant employer with extensive administrative facilities. It was to this base that the miserable crews were currently returning. Most of the *Starkotter* survivors headed for the seamen's infirmary.

Not dispassionately, from his second level office onshore, Admiral Cederstrom watched the wretched group make its way across the wharves. Many leant on ship-made crutches, while the more able-bodied carried friends in litters or supported each other in pairs that limped along. Casualties of war were expected, but not for the first or last time he wondered, "How many sailors on this ship have died or would be dying from the dreaded scurvy?"

Eventually the ship's captain and surgeon approached his office to provide their report. It wasn't dignified in any way, being similar to those which had arrived with all the other vessels in his command. Defeat after months at sea fighting the Russians, accompanied by the normal injuries and raging sickness, had left the sailors demoralized and debilitated.

Cederstrom turned to his second in command and with ill-concealed irritation said: "Set up a dinner meeting tonight, Lars. I want the chief doctors and head nurse from the infirmary, and invite Admiral Sir James Saumarez of the Royal British Navy and his chief surgeon to come along. Make it clear this is an invitation not to be denied. It's way past time we addressed this devastating sickness problem with renewed vigour and greater urgency."

With the food dishes cleared and cigars alight, the admiral raised the topic of scurvy and emphasized his concern by saying he regarded it as the most important issue currently facing his command. He sought advice first from the infirmary representatives, who emphasized the need for cleanliness and isolation, believing the disease was transmitted by touch from person to person. Under the admiral's penetrating questions, with insistence on knowing numbers of patients admitted and dismissed whether dead or alive, it became clear that while this treatment seemed to help contain the disease, it was no cure.

The Anglo-Swedish alliance had provided fifteen Royal Navy ships to help defend the territory, but they lay idle while King Charles XIII prevaricated on where to place his troops across the country. When asked for his opinion on the scurvy issue, the Fleet Physician, an Irishman named John Jamison, explained that he followed the ancient doctrine of the English physician James Lind who, way back in 1747, had advocated adding a heavy intake of citrus fruits, particularly oranges and lemons, to the usual shipboard diet. When the period at sea outlasted the time that perishable fruits and vegetables could be stored, the Navy turned to using lime juice. Lime juice and fresh fruits and vegetables were now a mandatory part of onboard diets and had been highly effective, not only in preventing scurvy, but in curing it in the few cases that still arose. Jamison agreed with the need for enforced personal cleanliness among soldiers and sailors but was not convinced that the disease was transmitted from man to man. His recommendation to the admiral and his lieutenants present was that all scurvy sufferers in the infirmary be immediately placed on a high-citrus diet.

Jamison had treated Admiral Nelson's wounds at the victorious Battle of Trafalgar in 1805 and on return to England had studied to be a physician at Edinburgh University, graduating with a Doctorate of Medicine in 1807 before rejoining the Navy, where he was held in high esteem.

Cederstrom considered his suggestion, and realized there was little physical risk in testing it. The main problem would be the support of his comrades and dealing with their enormous, if misplaced, pride. Having a foreigner try to solve the massive problem would not be well received. Deep down he had to admit failure on the part of the Navy doctors to date. It galled but, swallowing his own pride and believing in what he had just heard, he asked if Jamison would be willing to supervise the treatment of the affected sailors at the Swedish Navy headquarters in Karlskrona on the southeast coast.

Jamison agreed and stayed behind as the Navy ships returned to Britain.

The city of Karlskrona, two hundred overland miles and three hundred fifty nautical miles from Gothenburg, is spread over 30 islands in the eastern part of the Blekinge archipelago, the most southern of the Swedish archipelagos. The city was founded in 1680 when the Royal Swedish Navy relocated from the Stockholm area to Trossö Island, which had up until then been used chiefly for farming and grazing. At the time Sweden was the dominant military power in the Baltic Sea region, but needed a better strategic location against Denmark, since southern parts of Sweden had been conquered only a few decades before. Also, while previously located in Stockholm, the Swedish fleet tended to get stuck in the ice during winter, and hence was moved south.

The islands had a very strategic position with short sailing distances to the German and Baltic provinces. Karlskrona grew quickly, and by 1750 it had about ten thousand inhabitants, becoming one of the biggest cities in the country. Most of the baroque buildings from the era remain standing today.

Jamison reported to General Admiral Johan Puke at Naval headquarters. Although Puke was a supporter of the planned medical treatment, within the Naval command at large there were many doubters and indeed opponents who thought it would be a waste of money and effort and who constructed various administrative obstacles to thwart the new 'experiment.' Many of the administrative impediments were pure fabrications with little justification. Having a foreigner lead the effort insulted the pride many officers felt about their own capabilities, just as Admiral Cederstrom had predicted.

To his dismay, Jamison found that there were over three thousand sailors sick with the disease, ensconced in public and naval hospitals. The number affected had not been mentioned back in Gothenburg, and only now did he gain a far better understanding of the seriousness of the Swedish Navy's concern. It also made him incredibly angry as he realized he was overwhelmingly short-handed. Had he known in advance, he would have insisted that more assistant surgeons off the ships should stay and work with him. He made his displeasure well known, but there was no way the Navy could spare a ship to track down the British fleet and bring extra help back.

Jamison had his own pride, as well as faith in the treatment proposed, and the natural high energy levels of a born leader. At nearly six feet tall with a prolific beard and moustache, smooth skiined face, and high forehead above intelligent, piercing eyes, he shouldered the shock and anger and went to work. Tirelessly he visited many of the hospitals personally and immediately imposed stringent conditions for scurvy treatment by adding carefully calculated and measured amounts of local and imported citrus fruits to diets of patients in different phases of the disease. Stages and symptoms of the disease were categorized so that sailors ensconced in infirmaries in other ports could also benefit from the appropriate levels of supplements and treatment. He worked from morning to night, continually encouraging the few doctors willing to follow him in the massive 'experiment,' as the locals viewed it.

It didn't take long for positive impacts to be observed. Within four weeks a dramatic change took place for many. Shattered bones, lost teeth, and deformed joints could not be readily reversed, repaired, or replaced, but the incidence of bleeding in gums and eyes receded and pink flesh started to replace ugly damaged skin on hands, legs, faces, and particularly in the mouth. Moreover, patients everywhere simply felt better as the chemicals in the citrus juices overtook the disease itself.

Garth Sjovold and Sven Olsson had been admitted to the same ward in Gothenburg and both benefitted. They knew their lives would never be the same as before they enlisted, but they had survived and would work their farms again. They started to feel like men again, as opposed to walking shadows, and both rejoiced in their improvement. When finally discharged, they looked each other in the eyes and hugged for a long time. Each knew he could face the future with head high, and that returning to family was now something to look forward to. *"Må Gud vara med dig"* was voiced almost simultaneously as they waved goodbye, knowing they might never see the other again except in memories.

Not every sailor got better, as some were simply too far gone to be rehabilitated, but with detailed attention and measurement it was clear that the change in diet was a major success. The news spread quickly throughout the land and critics were silenced as the positive results mounted and the findings of the 'experiment' became unquestionable. Formal changes in onboard ship rations were soon prescribed.

As a result of Jamison's outstanding contribution and unswerving devotion to the welfare of the nation's sailors, the grateful Swedish king honoured the Irish physician by making him a Knight of the Order of Gustavus Vasa. Gustavus Vasa was King of Sweden from 1523 until his death in 1560. He was initially elected after leading the Swedish revolt against Danish rule, and was recognized as having united and pacified the country and established Lutheranism as the state religion. It was a highly prestigious award with which Jamison was bestowed. The results vindicated all he had predicted, and initial grudging respect from officials and doctors turned to outright adulation.

So recognized, Jamison returned to England triumphant, but it wasn't until four years later in 1813 that his work in Sweden was made public. He was then knighted by the Prince Regent, who later became King George IV. Sir John was subsequently appointed Inspector of Naval Hospitals and Fleets. It was as if he had simply done his duty as expected and should receive no special acknowledgment. It was the work of influential friends, however, that ensured his almost single-handed feat was appropriately rewarded at home, especially in light of the recognition abroad.

Sir John had been born thirty seven years earlier, in 1776, in Carrickfergus, County Antrim, on the northeast coast of Ireland.

Carrickfergus' history dates back to the sixth century when Fergus, the son of Erc of Armoy, left the province of Ulster to form a kingdom in Scotland. Upon returning to Ulster some time afterwards, his ship ran aground on a volcanic dyke by the shore, which became loosely known as "Carraig Fhearghais"—the rock of Fergus. The village became an inhabited town shortly after 1170, when the Anglo-Norman knight John de Courcy invaded Ulster, established his headquarters in the area, and built Carrickfergus Castle on the "rock of Fergus" in 1177. The castle, which is the most prominent landmark of Carrickfergus, is widely known as one of the best-preserved Norman castles in Ireland. Besieged in turn by the Scots, Irish, English, and French, the castle played an important military role until 1928. It was strategically useful, with three-quarters of the castle perimeter surrounded by water, although that changed over time with land reclamation.

Sir John's father, Thomas Jamison, was of Ulster-Scots Presbyterian descent, born in the seaside village of Ballywalter on the Ards Peninsula, County Down, in early 1753. For generations, the Jamisons had made their living from farming or from the sea, but Thomas excelled as a pupil at his parish school and had the initiative to choose a different path forward. The village had little to offer Thomas' fertile imagination and ambition, so early in life he moved away to County Antrim, married a local lass named Rebecca, fathered John and two daughters, Mary and Jane, and studied to be a surgeon, entering the British Navy in 1780.

In 1786 Thomas was assigned as surgeon's mate on *HMS Sirius* in the First Fleet headed to Australia to establish antipodean penal colonies destined to accommodate the growing population of criminals at home. The main colony was planned for Sydney where Governor Phillip, commander of the fleet, landed in January 1788.

From the wilderness, and between fights with the indigenous aborigines, the soldiers carved out a makeshift camp and gradually extended it to a few buildings for storage and administration. From virgin bushland they created a village with tracks for roadways, pastures for animals, a barracks for soldiers and prisoners alike, vegetable gardens, a jetty, and a chapel, and they harnessed a local water supply. It was tough going and for months prisoners were housed in open tent land camps, working in gangs at creating civil infrastructure during the day.

Two months after arrival, Governor Phillip sent a tiny detachment of guards, convicts, and naval personnel, including Thomas Jamison, to Norfolk Island, a speck in the charts of the Pacific Ocean approximately one thousand miles northeast of Sydney, to create an ancillary colony. Sized at thirteen square miles and undulating with peaks up to one thousand and fifty feet high, once again civilization was to be carved out of nothingness. The colony had to become self-sufficient. Jamison, although unhappy with his posting, helped the island commandant, Lieutenant King, make it happen. One didn't argue with Naval command.

The island colony became a very tough, incredibly unpleasant venue for convicts. Well beyond immediate Sydney supervision, convicts were forced into hard manual labour to create the settlement. As in Sydney, everything had to be created from scratch, land cleared and tilled for crops, pens and paddocks built for animals, water sources tamed and managed, roads and buildings established. Punishment was severe, with stories of convicts receiving over one thousand lashes in a three-year period for disobedience, malingering, unproductive work, and insolent attitudes. Free settlers beyond the military did not venture to Norfolk Island until all penal activity had ceased many years later.

The only communication with Sydney was via ship and visits were few and far between. The remoteness of the island however offered up certain positive aspects of life for non-convicts. The guards, soldiers, and various officials were able to pursue their own interests more easily than in Sydney due to the relatively small size of the contingent in place and the capability to expediently look after one another in the face of their isolated conditions of control over the criminal populace.

The lax arrangements of supervision and certain "understandings" among officers allowed easy uptake with female convicts. Lieutenant Philip Gidley King took up with Anne Inett, who bore him two sons named Norfolk and Sydney. Uxorious

Marine-Lieutenant Ralph Clark wrote to his wife Alicia about his dreams and longing for her but lived with a convict woman who produced a daughter named, most surprisingly, Alicia. Similarly, Jamison lived openly with Elizabeth Colley, who ended up having two boys and three girls by him. Colley, at age eighteen, had been convicted on 8 Dec 1784 at Old Bailey for receiving stolen clothing and had been sentenced to fourteen years in prison. She served two years in Middlesex gaol before being transported at age twenty-one to Australia on the *Lady Penrhyn,* one of the six convict transport ships in the First Fleet.

On 1 August 1797 she received a 'conditional pardon' and in 1801 she was marked *'gone to England'*—an unusual circumstance since most conditional pardons did not allow a return to the motherland. Her children were named Maria, born 4 August 1789; Thomas, born 24 November 1790; Elizabeth, born 28 March 1793; Harriet born 22 December 1794; and an unnamed son most likely born in 1796.

Another example of self-preservation on Norfolk Island was that of John Griffiths. He was appointed as a marine serving in the company of Captain James Meredith in Plymouth and had arrived in Sydney January 1788, aged twenty-eight, on the *Friendship* with the First Fleet. Sent to Norfolk, John eventually took up with Jane Thompson, born in Manchester, and who, at age eighteen, had been sentenced at York Quarter Sessions in April 1787 for seven years and transported on the *Neptune.* Part of the Second Fleet, this convict ship with over four hundred prisoners arrived in Sydney 27 June 1790.

John leased sixty acres on Norfolk and grew grain, which he sold to the local government stores. By 1806 he and Jane had been back in Sydney for ten years and were raising three boys and two girls: Robert, born in England to Jane; plus triplets John, Elizabeth, and William, born in 1795; and Mary, born in 1800. Unfortunately, mother Jane died in 1813 aged forty-four. Six years later John married Bridget Holland in Castlereagh, where he worked in the area as a sawyer. Females were a lot more scarce in the colonies than men, and were able to be somewhat selective in choosing mates. In fact, that was a relative situation as many of the men were not particularly attractive in habits, practices, values, or looks due to their treatment as criminals. But lone women were potential prey to sexually deprived men and in some sense choosing a partner was as much for protection as it was for company and support.

Convicts 'rehabilitated' from Norfolk Island often had trouble assimilating back into the Sydney colony. Most were seriously hardened and bitter, and formed consistently similar bonds in vouching for each other's characters and alibis when accused of further crimes. Many explained how they would rather be hung than be returned to Norfolk where cruelty was the norm for convicts.

At the other extreme, non-convicts with any self-initiative profited from their position. Thomas Jamison provided an example for all. Not only endowed with medical, sailing, and leadership skills, he also had a shrewd business brain. He was able to enrich himself by trading in pork, wheat, and, later, Indian sandalwood and alcohol. In fact, this trading was done partly in defiance of regulations applying to crown employees, which were hard to enforce in the remote location. Other officers also benefitted from illicit entrepreneurial efforts.

Recalled to Sydney in 1799, Thomas took a year's leave and returned to England, where he cultivated a set of influential patrons. As a result, he was appointed Surgeon-General of New South Wales where, on return, his medical skills shone. Among his accomplishments he published Australia's first medical paper, set up a process of qualification for would-be surgical doctors, and led a dedicated medical team which performed the colony's first successful vaccination against smallpox. In recognition of his broad range of accomplishments and contributions, in 1805 he received a one-thousand-acre grant of land on the Nepean River, west of Sydney, where he raised livestock and grew crops using assigned convict labor. He leased a townhouse in central Sydney as a city residence.

Thomas was appointed as a magistrate and while serving in that capacity participated in a series of maritime trading ventures, again in open defiance of government regulations which prohibited public officials from engaging in mercantile enterprises such as the lucrative rum trade. This time his transgressions weren't ignored. In retaliation, Governor Bligh, of mutiny-on-the-*Bounty* fame, refused Jamison permission in 1806 to return again to England to bring his family out, and in 1807 worsened things, through his overzealous penchant for discipline, by removing Jamison from the magistracy. Later that same year with great foresight Jamison acquired more land at George's River and South Creek for a total of twenty-three hundred acres.

In 1808, while his first-born son, John, was busy rehabilitating Swedish sailors, Thomas and other disaffected colonists joined forces with the New South Wales Corps to arrest and expel Bligh from Government House in a military coup d'état that became known as the Rum Rebellion. Massive bitterness over Bligh's disciplinary behavior, as on the *Bounty*, led to the coup. Afterwards, Jamison served as the Collector of Customs and Excise in the colony's temporary, rebel government. He was also given back his seat on the magistrates' bench.

Consistent with past behavior, Thomas had established a relationship with another female convict, who had arrived on the *William Pitt* 14 April 1806. Her trial and seven-year conviction had taken place at the Somerset Assizes on 11 Aug 1804. Through mispronunciation of her name in the embarkation port of Falmouth she was listed as Susannah Please. After she landed in Australia, her name was corrected to Sarah Place. She bore Jamison a son, Thomas Tristan, on 31 January 1808. He was baptized at St. Philip's Church, Sydney, two years later on 19 Aug 1810.

Jamison left Sydney for London in 1809 but fell ill the following year and died 25 January 1811. His biggest regret was that he was unable to testify against Governor Bligh in English court. His Australian estate passed entirely to his legitimate son, Sir John.

Thomas' widow, Rebecca, lived until 1838 back in County Antrim in Ireland on a government pension of thirty pounds per year. Elizabeth Colley was left twenty pounds, and Sarah Place enough to look after her son Thomas Tristan back in Australia.

The great man was buried in the graveyard of the Anglican Church of St Mary, Paddington Green, London. The graveyard was remodeled and turned into a park during Victorian times so, regretfully, no public memorial of his life and deeds now exists.

2. *Sydney 1814 – 1822*

The *Broxbornebury* crashed into another fifteen-foot wave and the bow lifted up and slammed down again. Timbers creaked and the wind moaned outside the cabin window. Judith Milward turned to her companion and once again asked nervously, "Are you sure we'll survive? This is the worst storm by far. I'm scared. Hold me tight."

The other hundred and twenty female convicts and the hordes of infants shrieked and cried in the space below decks. They clung to the stanchions and to one another, feeling every bone-shaking crunch the ship produced. None of the adults were sailors who well knew from experience that the ship could withstand much more than the human body. Two months ago most of the women and older girls had all been ensconced in dungeon cells in various English city gaols, and while those cells were in many ways intolerable with their lack of light, mold on the walls, and primitive sanitation, they were at least stationary. The walls didn't move and the only sounds among them were the whimpering of those being beaten or fornicating with guards or crying for whatever reason. Nature's winds didn't penetrate far below ground although the damp from the rains did and the smell of human waste never went away.

What was worse, some of the convict women now wondered, the cells they'd vacated, or this under-deck hole they'd been locked into that moved up and down and rolled side to side with its stifling air and claustrophobic environment? Even though they'd been at sea well over two months since leaving England, they had endured a slow voyage encountering numerous squalls en route. Some women still got seasick when the boat's motion became violent, adding to the unpleasantness of their holding space. Pregnant women suffered most. Two had already given birth and one baby had died almost immediately, being confined to the deep in a sad deck-side service.

The only redeeming feature for the women was that the *Broxbornebury* was relatively new, having been built just two years earlier as a seven-hundred-and-twenty-ton transport ship, albeit equipped with fourteen gun placements for protective purposes. There were no male convicts on this special ship, although a number of important male passengers were in the cabins topside. A few opportunistic females had established relationships with selected male crewmen and passengers, hoping their sexual favours might be rewarded on arrival in the penal colony. For these females, the price of survival was between their legs. For others, religious beliefs, faithfulness to husbands left behind, and traditional senses of decency and behavior kept them chaste.

Among the sexually favored passengers was Sir John Jamison, who pronounced his name "Jemison" in the Irish manner. His sailing experience stood him in good stead and one more time as the ship pitched awkwardly, he reached for his nubile friend Judith and reassured her. "This ship can stand far worse seas than this, my dear. Have faith, Captain Pitcher said we'd be clear in about two more hours based on his glimpses of the horizon ahead. I think there are ways we can fill in the time till then, don't you agree?"

On 14 January 1814 at the age of nineteen Judith Milward had been tried and convicted for stealing food in Devon. She spent a month in the local gaol as part of her seven-year sentence and was transferred to the *Broxbornebury* just before it set sail from Gravesend on 22 February 1814. With a roving eye and bold initiative, she identified Sir John early in the voyage as a promising candidate to help her at the other end of the voyage. She pursued him with charm and guile in the few opportunities that presented themselves, her innocent looks and childish figure making her very attractive in his and many other male eyes. Bedding her had required little persuasion or effort on Sir John's part, and he was happy to be provided extra comforts on the long trip.

The *Broxbornebury* was destined to have an unusual trip to the Antipodes. Fourteen months earlier, on 30 November 1812, a sister transport ship, the *Emu*, under the command of Lieutenant Alexander Bissett, was captured in the Atlantic by the American privateer *Holkar* during the British-American War of 1812–1814.

The *Emu* was subsequently taken to New York as a 'prize' and sold there. The captain, twenty-two crew, and forty-nine women convicts on board were put ashore at Porto Grande on the island of St Vincent in the Cape Verde Islands on 17 January 1813. The castaways were eventually rescued after twelve months by the crew of the *Isabella* and returned to Britain. The convict women were not permitted to land, however, but were placed on a hulk in Portsmouth Harbour and subsequently transferred on board the transport *Broxbornebury* to continue their voyage. These women had endured more than most other convicts would even hear about, let alone experience, and were unique in the transportation annals of female convicts.

One hundred fifty-six days after leaving London the *Broxbornebury* anchored off the Quay in Sydney Cove. It was 28 July 1814 and it was a cold day that greeted the convicts and passengers. They'd left their homeland in the northern hemisphere winter only to arrive in this strange new place in a southern hemisphere winter. Was there no forgiveness? Furthermore, the end of their voyage was almost as contrary as the start. Earlier, on the same day as they arrived, the *Surrey*, a convict ship built to carry two hundred male passengers, had also arrived after a stop in Rio de Janeiro. A typhus epidemic on board had killed thirty-six of the convicts, together with the surgeon, first and second mates, boatswain, two seamen, and four of the guard. Sydney authorities immediately placed all the survivors under a strict quarantine in a camp on the "North Shore" of Port Jackson, opposite the Quay.

Apprehensions amongst crew, convicts, and passengers on the *Broxbornebury* ran high when they learned of the proximity of the disease-affected ship anchored nearby. Quarantine restrictions on the *Surrey* were lifted within a couple of weeks but the restrictions on the shore camp lasted for some time. The *Broxbornebury* on its voyage had suffered only four deaths, two being children, amongst its hundred and twenty female convicts, which was a typical death rate for such a trip. Passengers were distraught however at the thought that after surviving their ignominious trip, they were now at risk from disease in a stationary but unknown environment.

Unusual events associated with the *Broxbornebury* continued even later when she planned to leave port on her return trip. A number of the seaman had deserted ship. They were named in the newspaper as Cornelius McGuire, John Simmons, Thomas Lewis, Aaron Walters, Alexander Grant, Thomas Davis, James Sullivan, Andrew Angel, James Ryan, John Morris, Thomas Hunt, Nicholas Johnson, and Samuel McDonald. Four pounds per head was offered for their 'delivery' back to the ship's commander. How many returned is unknown, but on the way out of the harbour Captain Pitcher forced four men into a boat rowed by the Second Mate Mr. Owen and abandoned them on Sydney's North Head. They were later rescued by a passing fisherman.

Tough actions were clearly applied on the high seas.

Sir John was one of the more fortunate arrivals in Sydney since he had access to income from his father Thomas' accounts and was able to immediately rent a town house with a view of the harbour on Bunker's Hill, near Dawes Point. Due to Thomas' shrewd investments he found himself the owner of several grazing and city properties as well as a number of successful trading businesses. Others also benefitted from Sir John's wealth. He had brought out a steward with him named John Stilwell, whom he employed as manager of a couple of hotels, including the Westmoreland Arms, that he owned in the city. He also hired two of the convict women who were on the *Broxbornebury*, a Jane Jones who later married John Stilwell, and a Catherine Barnes. Catherine was convicted on 3 May 1813 in Lancaster, and had waited for transportation a year less than had Jane Jones in London. Jane was only seventeen when desperation had driven her and her fifteen-year-old companion, Ann Rogers, to climb the mews dunghill at 7:00 a.m., break a window in the pub, clamber in, and steal not just food, but also money from the till. The two girls were intercepted by a beadle who was amazed at their haul since it included a chicken, four loaves of bread, five eggs, a saucepan and cover, butter, cheese, two knives, two forks, two plates, a spoon, a basin, a tinder-box, and a wooden drawer containing 140 pennies, 2,124 half-pennies, and 463 farthings! Not the usual set of possessions for young girls of the times!

Jamison's need for variety in feminine company and benefits of the flesh led him to begin an affair with Catherine Kean, another convict from the *Broxbornebury* who had caught Sir John's eye. Judith Milward had served her purpose in the months at sea and Sir John needed a change. On 12 January 1813, at the age of nineteen, Catherine had been tried and convicted in London for having a forged pound note in her possession and using it for purchases of food. She spent a year in Middlesex gaol as part of her fourteen-year sentence and was moved to the *Broxbornebury* just before it set sail from Gravesend. Catherine also became one of the more fortunate arrivals, as she was invited to share Sir John's dwelling as his de facto wife and mistress of the house. Most of the other women convicts were sent to the Female Factory at Parramatta to make clothes for fellow male and female convicts.

At her registration with Australian immigration authorities Catherine had insisted that her last name was Cain, not Kean, the latter being a poorly misinterpreted pronunciation of her name that had been recorded at her initial arrest. The spelling of her first name was also slightly erroneous. She wanted to start her new life properly with her correct name. While John caught up with the status of his father's estate which had been ably managed by his father's friends, Dr. D'Arcy Wentworth, Reverend Samuel Marsden, and Dr. Charles Throsby, Catherine, now known as Catharine Cain, spent time learning the ins and outs and details of the city.

From that time on, after showing little interest in continuing to follow the medical profession, Sir John concentrated on building up his existing estates and acquiring further land holdings. His final deed as a medical man had been to help assess the state of disease on the *Surrey* and to help prepare medicines for treatment of prisoners thereon. But there his medical interest rested. Power, prestige, and wealth in the form of city and country land ownership, cattle and sheep raising, and merchant trade were far more exciting and rewarding.

John had social aspirations and soon was a semi-regular companion of Governor Lachlan Macquarie at Government House. Outside the city, he often visited the dwelling his father had built on the banks of the Nepean, south of Penrith. Sir John named the estate there 'Regentville', in honour of King George IV, the former Prince Regent, who had knighted him.

After William Cox had completed a crude roadway over the Blue Mountains in January 1815, the governor decided to travel the rough road through to Bathurst. The road was a truly significant accomplishment for the colony. For years the Blue Mountains had been a natural barrier to the west of Sydney. Many expeditions had sought to find a route across them but all had given up in frustration. It wasn't until 1813 that Blaxland, Wentworth, and Lawson finally forged a trail all the way to the plains beyond. Their trail and the subsequent road opened up the fertile west for agriculture and was a major milestone in the development of the new country. Its significance was readily recognized by the Governor who anticipated that his trip across the mountains would encourage farmers and other free settlers to move and settle in the west. Accompanied by Sir John, the governor's party crossed the Nepean at Jamison's farm and the journey proper began at the government stockyards at Emu Plains. The beautiful Jamison Valley high up in the mountains was named after Sir John in recognition of his helpfulness. Though he and the governor were friends at the time, the relationship faltered later on.

Although Sydney Town was established as a penal colony, its nature gradually changed as convicts served out their sentences and an increasing number of free settlers began to arrive. It became more of a 'frontier town' and gradually various institutions of trade and commerce began to emerge. Due to the changing economic climate, one of the earliest needs was for a bank. In the absence of financial institutions and a local stable monetary system, rum, promissory notes, British Treasury bills, foreign coins, and barter were all used as currency. Recognizing the need to have a stable financial system, in February 1817, Governor Macquarie signed a charter of incorporation which established the Bank of New South Wales. This was Australia's first financial institution. Sir John became one of the founders of this bank, which survives today under the Westpac name. Initially the bank leased premises in Macquarie Place, Sydney, from Mary Reibey, an ex-convict turned businesswoman, and opened for business on 8 April 1817. It did not, however, act as a savings bank, and although it lent in mortgages from the beginning, this lending function was minimal, because of the uncertainty of the status of the land titles offered as security. No matter its conservative policies, its very existence added financial stability to the country and helped expand trade, commerce, and farming over the years.

As with all societies, and especially infant ones, opportunists and con men prevailed. Once convicts got their pardons and a trade infrastructure was established between Sydney and England, many enterprising individuals were quick to envision new money-making opportunities. Certainly, not all of them had serious criminal capabilities. But on the long sea voyages, even prisoners who were less hardened learnt well from those who were more notorious.

One of the flourishing trades that became prominent on Sydney streets was that of jewelry shops. Many upper middle class ladies were able to find amazing quality offerings at remarkable prices, far below what they would have had to pay back home. The reason, of course, was that most of the items were stolen, and it was a lot easier to get rid of them in Sydney than it was in London. Other merchandise was much bulkier and more costly to transport, so jewelry stood out as one of the best bargains on Sydney streets for years.

Commerce grew in multiple areas, especially those on which life was dependent, such as food, wine, clothing, basic furniture, and tools. But the sparkle of diamonds was to be found in many a chest of drawers under madam's necessities. With Sir John's wealth at hand his partner Catharine indulged and purchased numerous jewels to choose from to display at the various at-home parties and galas the couple held.

On 26 November 1815 the first of three children was born. Unfortunately, the little girl, named Sophia Rebecca, with the name Rebecca possibly tying back to Sir John's mother, died two years later on 8 February 1817.

Two months before Sophia's birth, the transport ship *Baring* had arrived on 7 September 1815 with two hundred ninety-eight male convicts on board. It took John Thomas Campbell, the governor's secretary, two days to muster the convicts on board and complete his documentation. And one week after arrival, the convicts were disembarked and marched to the local gaol to be inspected and addressed by Governor Macquarie. In the meantime, their trades and conduct reports had been examined closely, and the assignment lists made out. Fifty-seven of the "mechanics," or tradesmen, and thirty of the labourers were to be retained for employment by the government; one hundred forty-one were to be sent to the magistrates at Parramatta, Liverpool, and Windsor for distribution to landholders who had applied for them. But some were set aside by the governor himself.

It was the era of patronage, and the gentry of the colony, rather than apply for convict servants through the magistrates as was the rule, would approach the governor directly for convicts with special skills such as ploughmen or carpenters or cooks. Joseph Douglass, a Scot who had been caught stealing in 1814 and sentenced to seven years, was on the list of three labourers from the *Baring* to be assigned by the governor directly to Sir John. Joseph eventually became the only one of the three to remain in Jamison's service for the entire period of his servitude.

Since 1804, convicts assigned to settlers had been regulated as to working hours and the amount of work to be completed during those hours. They were paid an annual wage of ten pounds including clothing, and then paid at set rates for extra work beyond the stipulated weekly amount. Sir John supported these regulations and observed:

'By being well trained to perform such labour the very nature of the profligate seems to change, and many of them discover a new pride at the acquired knowledge of being able to provide for themselves by honest industry.'

Joseph Douglass was employed as a specialist plough and seedman and was soon saving his wages for the day when he could set up on his own block of land, and to have his wife and five children, who'd been left behind, join him. His first break came with the announcement in 1817 that free passages might be available for wives and children of deserving convicts. Wives had been discouraged from arriving since at least 1814 because so many of them and their families in the colony were destitute and supported on the public purse. Joseph, with the help of Sir John, was able to provide the necessary proof of income and in March 1819 the governor's dispatch to London named Joseph as capable of supporting Mary and his five children, who were then living "at Mr. Morrison's, Saintfield, Downpatrick, Ireland." While Sir John had strict rules for the management of convicts placed at his farm estate there was a compassionate side that endeared him to many.

There was a marked dichotomy in his interactions with people. On one hand he avidly cultivated relationships with government officials, clergymen, ships captains, judges, magistrates, merchantmen, and wealthy free settlers. It appears these were primarily of economic and political value as they helped Sir John achieve positions of power and interest, and at the same time allowed him to more easily attain both convict assignments and the goods that he wanted for his estate.

On the other hand when he was looking for labourers he made no distinction between convicts and free settlers. He hired workers on the basis of skills and attitude. Status was irrelevant. Convicts could have seven years, fourteen years, or life terms. It mattered not. As long as they served him faithfully Sir John supported his workers. If they committed a crime, however, he had no hesitation in using the police and the law to respond. Perhaps he realized, better than others, that many of the original crimes were petty in nature and that transportation from the homeland was more of a convenience for judges and gaolers than a real solution to the advent of crime. The snobbishness and vanity of the middle and upper class population back home in regarding all criminals as villainous, corrupt, undesirable heathens was not something he agreed with or supported. He knew that in general they were human beings who had ended up in poverty, desperate to try and support themselves in the presence of a calamitous economic and social environment.

In highly personal relationships with women, despite the ready availability of single daughters of high officials, he always chose convicts for mates. Perhaps it was because they were more dependent on him for their well-being, whereas social debutantes from wealthy families might not have been as tolerant of his roving eye. Also the latter were more likely to have at their discretion political sway and family influence that could limit his free will. Historically, his father's way of life had probably also set examples of behavior that Sir John felt could readily be followed. Having given up practicing his professional capabilities of sailing and doctoring, he instead started to pursue a free-spirited lifestyle that combined that of the landed gentry with that of the wealthy playboy.

The explorer interest in Sir John, however, helped finance several trips of discovery in the state of New South Wales. In 1818, at his own expense, he led the first expedition to travel through the Warragamba gorge, up the Warragamba River to the Cox's River junction. The boat they embarked in was only twelve feet long with a five-foot beam. Two miles from the starting point of the gorge they saw a small stream of running water which was named Glen Brook. Years later a small town named Glenbrook developed a few miles away. A month after his return Sir John sent out another party, consisting of his botanist collector, Thomas Jones; and three natives, Bob, Joe, and Jack, to trace the Cox's River back to the Warragamba. Select natives were often used by government officials for tracking and exploration purposes. Over time various merchants tried to use natives for labour but the 'walkabout' notion that was culturally inherent in the aborigine culture would suddenly take over and the merchant would find his workers gone from their jobs, back scouring the land they'd been raised in.

A few miles after setting out on this trip the group came across a savage tribe of Condanora aborigines. The encounter ended peacefully, although two of John's native helpers felt they were at risk of being cannibalized during the exchange.

On 28 January 1819 a second daughter, Harriet Eliza Jamison, was born to John and Catharine. Nearly two decades later, on Thursday 20 April 1837 at St. James Church, Harriet married a William John Gibbes, son of Major Gibbes, the Collector of Customs. This was a very special occasion as His Excellency the Governor Major-General Sir Richard Bourke honoured the bride and bridegroom with his presence at the nuptials, and, along with his staff, dined with Sir John in the evening. In the early years after marriage, Harriet produced a number of children, many of whom died as infants, the one surviving son, William Charles Valentine, being born much later on 11 March 1848.

By the early 1820s John Jamison was well-renowned as a prominent citizen in the colony. He acquired more land by grant and purchase and extended his Penrith estate. Back in Sydney he received a grant of a major block of land bounded by the Military Barracks, George Street, Charlotte Place, and the Scots Kirk. Jamison replaced the existing dilapidated buildings there and shortly after built for himself a very distinguished, large, and modern two-storey townhouse on the northern side of a street that was added and named after him. The various properties around his own returned him a handsome income through rents and land sales.

As Australia's first titled free settler, de facto, he became head of the fledgling country's social pecking order. When not touring his outlying properties and residence in Sydney he occasionally give a ball with supper at his new city house. Up to one hundred and forty people would be served in one large room, with carriages organized to bring guests to and from the mansion.

All the servants were convicted felons, a situation that many attendees who originated in English society found uncomfortable. But dancing and drinking would continue all night and their concerns would eventually dissipate. Becoming an acquaintance of Sir John was a prestigious mark of passage for would-be socialites.

A charismatic man of high intelligence, and liberal social ideals, he was quickly becoming an emerging patriot for the development of the country.

3. Professional Services

Back in Britain the newspapers, encouraged by bureaucratic officials, emphasized how more and more despicable criminals were being sent to Botany Bay and how it was serving the purpose of ridding the country of the worst type of people who were the scourge of society—thieves, rapists, murderers, vagrants, forgers, pickpockets, and prostitutes. Crime and poverty from overcrowding was finally being relieved. Regular citizens would soon see the benefits.

There was one main difference between prisoners at home and those sent to the Antipodes. The latter had to build their own gaols, in a primitive country beset by savage natives. Chain gangs and hard labour were the standard way of life. Even the detestable women sent there carried out His Majesty's will by making clothes and serving the military and convicts in baking and cooking. For the majority of British citizenry it was good riddance to the human vermin of the land—out of sight, out of mind.

The true story was that Governor Philip and his successors were bent on building a society in the new land, starting with a penal colony as the primary source of labour. The military personnel, along with select non-military persons, were busy planning a new town, setting the priorities for infrastructure and self-sufficiency. The families of these officials sent back contrary messages to relatives. While Sydney did indeed manage a growing penal colony, there were some attractions in this land so far away that lent favorable comparisons with the situation back home. The sun shone brilliantly. There were no smokestacks polluting the sky with dense coal fumes, no dark, narrow crime-ridden alleys and thoroughfares; and there were oodles of land with acreage for agriculture being given away to those who could justify a capability to work the land or who deserved it for other reasons, and abundant fresh water and fertile soil. Flowers and trees grew in abundance and the fauna was amazingly unique and attractive. After initial confrontations, and mostly minor ones in newly discovered country areas, the natives were not a serious problem.

In fact, some had become helpful to the administration for tracking and leading explorers to new finds. Above all, even for convicts who behaved well, there was opportunity in many areas of endeavour. As well, the first marriages between convicts and free settlers had taken place, adding an extra dimension to the local society.

Religious sects were sending out increasing numbers of ministers and leaders to build churches and to carry out missionary work among the natives. The government was demanding more and more supplies of increasing variety, and the merchants sourcing them in England and Wales started to recognize that unforeseen growth was fueling this blessed change in fortune. Many enterprising merchants established Australian branches or signed up with representative agents as the new marketplace developed. The number of ships ferrying cargo but no convicts increased, and the volume of mail grew substantially. Reciprocally, the cargo ships were starting to take back to English ports vast quantities of high-quality wool and wheat, so a vibrant export/import trade began to flourish both at home and abroad. Slowly, quietly, messages of opportunity started to pervade the governmental and commercial segments of society. The government was signing up engineers and select scientists such as botanists and geologists as greater sophistication was needed in understanding the New South Wales environment and consequent building and infrastructure needs. Behind the commercial interests came the professional services providers—lawyers, doctors, accountants, architects etc. And way behind these were the artists of the times—painters, writers, musicians.

Southeast of London lies the village of Ewell. On 14 October 1793, five years after the First Fleet arrived in Sydney Cove, Henry Kitchen was born to parents Henry and Mary at their home on Church St. in Ewell. Henry, the father, had remarried in 1792 and was sixty years old when his son arrived. In various town historical writings he was variously described as builder, carpenter, and bricklayer—probably acting generally as a contractor, but particularly for bricklayer work on the Surrey Gaol and Sessions

House. In 1780 he undertook to erect a new gallery on the south side of St Mary's Church, paying for the work, but recouping his costs by selling extra pews. He built and furnished a new wing of the old Pest House in May 1781, and around 1786 published a collection of his own Gothic-style house designs. His last building, which became known as Dorset House, was completed in 1802, two years before his untimely death.

Son Henry studied under the respected and fashionable London architect James Wyatt. Henry later set up a practice at 36 St James's Place, and no doubt benefitted from those commissioning his designs in Ewell. Thomas Hercey Barritt and Thomas Calverley were neighbours and family acquaintances. Their buildings had been erected by 1814. By 23 April 1815, Henry Kitchen gained an appointment as Architect and Surveyor of the Norwich Union [Insurance] Company.

His mother, Mary, died on 13 July 1816 after a protracted illness. Later the same month, saddened, single, and alone, but captivated by the opportunities for building in New South Wales, he sailed from Cork as a free settler on the *Surry* bound for Australia. He had with him a letter of introduction to the Governor of the Colony from Lord Bathurst of Downing Street:

"Mr. Kitchen having my permission to proceed to the Colony under your Government, I am to desire that you will grant to him an allotment of Land corresponding to the amount of Capital which he is able to satisfy you he has the means of commanding for its Cultivation.

Mr. Kitchen having been regularly educated as a Surveyor and Architect may render himself useful to you if the services of such a Professional Person should be required in the Colony.

I have the honour to be
Bathurst"

Unfortunately, by the time Henry arrived in December 1816 Governor Lachlan Macquarie had already selected one of his convicts, with a record of achievement back in England, to the post of acting civil architect.

Henry advertised his services in the *Sydney Gazette* as follows:

> *"Mr. Kitchen, Architect and Surveyor, a late pupil of James Wyatt, Esq., Surveyor General of His Majesty's Board of Works, begs leave to acquaint Gentlemen and others connected with Building, that he is desirous of Engaging, upon moderate terms, in the superintendency and actual Management of Designs, whether for plain and agreeable Residences, Storehouses, Field and Road Improvements, or any other plans of Rural Oeconomy [Economy], or of Town Improvement.*
>
> *Mr. Kitchen, who has but recently arrived per the ship <u>Surry</u>, will be happy, previous to entering upon any actual Engagement to render every satisfaction to Gentlemen who may wish to favour him with their instructions, in a private conference, the result of which he has no doubt will be a confidence which will be his entire study to improve. - Apply 49, Philip Street."*

Henry was engaged for a variety of building projects, including in 1818 the design and erection of a church in Windsor. This and other works brought him to the attention of Sir John Jamison, who commissioned him very early in 1822 to build two new houses at his property in George St., Sydney. In March of that year Henry advertised in *The Sydney Gazette and New South Wales Advertiser* for stonemasons, bricklayers, and carpenters to apply for positions.

It would ultimately turn out that colonial architectural skills would be limited and competitive, with much criticism thrown between adversaries as to others' capabilities and style. Henry was given credit for doing more for Sir John than records ultimately ended up refuting. His work however brought out the best in other architects who became just as renowned.

Unfortunately, Henry did not fare well in his adopted country. It was still a primitive culture in some respects as evidenced by the fact that a year earlier on 10 April 1821 a bundle of dirty linen was stolen from his premises. Two women, Margaret Roach and Catherine Clarkson, were committed for stealing and receiving the goods, respectively. Henry was not well at the time, and his poor health never improved, to the point that he died 8 April 1822 just

after advertising for help to build Sir John's new houses.
He was buried in the Sandhills Cemetery, Sydney, the
inscription on his headstone reading

"HENRY KITCHEN ESQRE.,
Architect
formerly pupil of the justly celebrated JAMES WYATT, Esqre, deceased
Died April 8th 1822
Aged 29 Years"

4. A Country Estate

In mid-1823, Sir John embarked on a project so unique that it coloured not only his life, but also the lives of countless others for the next twenty years and beyond. Australia was still incredibly 'new.' The initial tents of the penal colony had been pegged in virgin bushland only thirty-five years earlier. City planning was still in its infancy. Infrastructure was being gouged out by chain gangs of convicts. Roads leading out of Sydney were rough and ready. New wharves and warehouses around Darling Harbour were under construction. Convicts were still pouring into the country along with more military personnel to manage them. Free settlers were in a minority, albeit growing. The first commercially licensed pub, as opposed to informal make-shift establishments, had just been approved. The Murrumbidgee River had recently been discovered. Crime was a major issue. Skirmishes with aborigines still took place.

Societal progress was definitely evident, with widely held recognition that the penal colony was slowly being transformed into a commercial town. But by any measures used in the old world, it was still a very early time in antipodean civilization.

Sir John stunned friends and acquaintances in high society by deciding to build a magnificent mansion at his property on the Nepean River, over thirty-five miles away from Sydney. This edifice, to be built of solid sandstone, would rival any building in the country, including Government House. The first stone was laid on Tuesday 9 September 1823. The fact that it was so far away from the hub of modern society and commerce was what was amazing to everyone. With the passing of Henry Kitchen, Sir John chose as architect ex-convict Francis Greenway, who had previously designed and built some of his Sydney houses in 1820 and 1821.

Francis was an architect "of some eminence" in Bristol. After becoming bankrupt he forged financial instruments, which landed him in Newgate prison for nearly two years before he was transported to Australia in 1814 on a fourteen-year sentence.

Because of his qualifications, however, he was soon given a Ticket of Leave and set up an architectural practice in George St. in Sydney Town. Among the buildings he designed were the Hyde Park Barracks, Government House, Macquarie Lighthouse, and what is considered to be his masterpiece, St James' Church, Sydney. And, of course, Sir John's mansion.

The Mulgoa Valley through which the Nepean River ran had the advantage of pockets of alluvial soil along the creek beds feeding into the river. Many prominent citizens, along with high-ranking military personnel, had been granted land in the region, and although they didn't necessarily reside there, it was clearly the 'country place in which to own land'. Sir John started clearing and cultivating his property some years before deciding to build there. Between 1804 and 1816 large acreages had been granted to the well-renowned merchant Simeon Lord, the Reverends Samuel Marsden and Robert Cartwright, and explorers Gregory Blaxland and William Cox, among others. Over time Sir John was to buy up many of these allotments, extending his own holdings immensely. He grew crops and vegetables, planted orchards, and stocked his fields with sheep, cows, pigs, goats, and horses.

His incredible wealth allowed him to achieve ends that others couldn't contemplate. He could afford to own the extensive acreage and at the same time live by the river. The cost of transport between Sydney and Penrith was of niggling concern relative to other expenditures. And by locating in the countryside he wouldn't be bothered by trifling demands on his time and presence as would be the case were he to stay in Sydney.

And so plans were prepared for the location and building of Sir John's mansion in prime agricultural territory. To the west rose the beautiful Blue Mountains, home to the vast Dharug tribe, guardian of yet undiscovered secret caves, valleys, waterfalls, and cliffs, as well as unnamed species of unique flora and fauna. The mountains were no longer an obstacle to opening up the interior of the country. Sir John's foresight saw trade increasing and his abode as a possible resting and trading post with its strategic position.

Prior to any thought of building his mansion Sir John had been diligently investing in the land he owned. His father's original home served as quarters for the various trips John made back and forth between Sydney and the property. Even this old house was a large building, with four fireplaces and a veranda all around, the overhang providing shade across doors and windows alike. There were a number of outbuildings, some attached, some separate, providing laundry, kitchen, and storage facilities. Stables were a little distance from the house, and a short walk away the river flowed gently by.

The river's source was actually some sixty miles south of Sydney whence it flowed northward through Camden, recognized for its importance as a wool fgrowing centre. Eight miles below the site of the old house, it was joined by the substantial Cox's River. Numerous creeks running downhill from the Blue Mountains added to the volume of clear fresh water. Fish abounded, and there were several small rowing boats that were frequently in use by fishermen bringing dinner home. Orderly lines of fence posts defined fields stretching to the river.

Throughout Sir John's first seven years of residence, hundreds of trees had been cut down and milled for various purposes, and the cleared land tilled and planted with crops and fruit trees. Paddocks had been formed for livestock and several different species of animals purchased and allowed to range in them.

Unskilled labourers had dug out trenches for the portage of water from the river to a pumping station and subsequent distribution to areas not served by creeks but reserved for the orchards and planned vineyards. The orchards were already providing a wide variety of fruits. A windmill was already in place to help pump water from the river and through the irrigation system.

Sir John's social interests and capabilities extended from Sydney to his country home. While visitors were far fewer here many official or otherwise significant travelers heading over the Blue Mountains were helped in some capacity including good meals, most likely the best they would experience for many days to come. In April 1822 the Hawkins family, recently arrived from England, set out from Sydney headed for Bathurst, one hundred and thirty-seven miles away. These were free settlers, eleven strong, traveling to take up Mr. Hawkins' appointment as commissariat storekeeper. After staying two nights at Government House in Parramatta they proceeded to the Nepean River but had to wait for new horses and carts to continue their journey through the mountains. They experienced further delays due to heavy rain soaking all their goods, which had to be dried out for a full day.

Out of the goodness of his heart Sir John, who had heard of their plight, provided a guard to watch some of their belongings and invited Mr. and Mrs. Hawkins to dinner. Mrs. Hawkins later wrote a letter home to her sister Ann in which she described the event as follows:

"Sir J. Jamison had invited a lady and two gentlemen to meet us. We partook of a sumptuous repast, consisting of mock-turtle soup, boiled fowls, round of beef, delicious fish of three kinds, curried duck, goose and wild-fowl, Madeira and Burgundy, with various liqueurs and English ale. I was delighted with his garden. The apples and quinces were larger than I ever saw them before, and many early trees of the former were again in blossom. The vines had a second crop of grapes, and fig trees a third crop. The peaches and apricots here are standing trees. He had English cherries, plums and filberts. These, with oranges, lemons, limes, and citrons, medlars. Almonds, rock and water melons, with all the common fruits of England: vegetables of all kinds, and grown at all seasons of the year, which shows how the climate is. The next morning Sir John came to see us off, and presented us with a quarter of mutton, a couple of fowls and some butter."

Now in late spring, on his current visit, Sir John and his seedsman, Joseph Douglass, rode slowly away from the old stables. The horses stepped warily along the makeshift road that paralleled the river, finally being reined in at Surveyor's Creek, a mile and a quarter away. They rested on the southern bank and Joseph pointed out the two closest fields beyond the stream. "See, m'lord, the wheat is now a foot tall, and I estimate we have five acres or so planted. The next field to the west is planted with rye, and is a little behind, but very healthy. We'll keep what we need to make flour and sell the remainder of both crops in Parramatta. Let's cross the creek and I'll show you the vegetable gardens beyond." In July Sir John had been appointed President of the Agricultural and Horticultural Society of New South Wales at the Society's inaugural meeting. The governor was asked to accept the office of Patron and Mr. Frederick Goulburn the Vice Patronage. Sir John relished his position, as he actively promoted the best practices of the times and shared his ideas, information, and results broadly. He had worked with Joseph on crop rotation, timing of seeding, fertilizing, and watering and constantly checked on results of new procedures and experiments.

"As I understand it, Joseph, this creek rises along the eastern edge of this crop area, runs south and then turns to the west, flowing in front of us here down to the Nepean. That way we have ready water on two boundaries and don't need to force manual irrigation, just use channels in the soil to distribute the water naturally to the fields."

"Aye, sir, that's close to the arrangement, and the location is almost perfect in that respect. What's more, the creek will also serve the tenant farms when they get established because if you look to the west about a quarter mile you'll see the creek turns to the north. Its course is sort of a U shape, and it joins the Nepean downstream a good mile away, outside your property line."

"OK, let's cross here and move on to the vegetable fields." So saying, Sir John slapped his horse's rump and waded into the slowly moving stream. "By the way, don't say too much about the tenant farms, Joseph. I'm not ready to advertise their availability fully yet because I want to make sure that the best land is used for my own produce first. You have served me long and faithfully and I'm happy for you to be the first to work some tenant acreage starting next month, for I know you will work it well. I will be hard pressed to find someone with as much experience to take your place. What is the latest on the potential timing of your family's arrival?"

"Lots of delays, sir, but we're thinking by spring of next year they should be here. I'll take time off to go down and meet them in Sydney. We'll see. The missus is very thankful for your recommendations and support, sir."

"Glad to have helped out. And while I think of it, let me ask a question. Have you seen any of those platypus creatures around here, Joseph? I've been in the colony eight years now but still haven't seen one. The descriptions I've heard make them sound very strange. We tried to find them on my trip over the Blue Mountains with the governor years ago, but I guess they are very shy, and have their burrows in protected spots. You ever see one, let me know."

"Of course, Sir John. With all the creeks traversing the estate you'd think there must be one or two around somewhere. I'll keep my eyes open and my ears tuned for any hints from the labourers and natives. Ah. Here we are. Potatoes and peas are the most advanced crops that you see in front of you. But further on we have carrots, onions, and cabbages. We won't go hungry, sir."

"Very good, Joseph. Tell me, since you've been camped out here managing the crops have we had any flooding from any of the creeks?"

"No, sir. On this side of the river there's not enough slope to the land nor enough rainfall to matter. On the other side the creeks run more steeply and the mountains get a lot more rain. I have seen the Nepean run much fuller, but your house is far enough away that even if it floods you won't be affected. There must be a lot of creeks upstream that feed into the river, methinks."

"Oh yes, I can assure you of that. When we went exploring into the Warragamba area back four years ago the banks were pockmarked with incoming streams. I don't think we'll run out of fresh water here, Joseph—which is one of the reasons I picked this spot. Sure is beautiful, isn't it?"

A lingering silence followed as each man retreated to his thoughts. A crow flew across their path, the beat of his wings stirring the heavy air. Minutes drifted by and finally Joseph brushed aside the shyness that had surprisingly overcome him.

"You know, where I lived back in Scotland, sir, I thought there was no prettier place on earth. The rolling hills, the moors, the lochs, the heather, little stone fences and quaint stiles, small clumps of trees scattered far between. I used to walk for miles just enjoying the serenity of the scenery. Me, my thoughts, my pipe, and m' dog, of course. Made me feel rich and content. Never was a city person, although that's where I got into trouble. Never ever thought much about Australia. It was just some place on the other side of the world. Until, of course, I learned I was to be sent there. Here, I mean.

"It certainly is different from where I grew up," he continued. "In many, many ways. Not just because I'm here at His Majesty's pleasure. If I were a free man I don't know that I'd want to migrate here as you have done, but I think in time the country will become very attractive. It's not even forty years old—the colony, that is— but already I see more free men and women helping transform Sydney into a real town. It's not just the centre of a penal colony anymore. Men like yourself are changing things for the better."

Sir John smiled. "That's quite a speech, Joseph. And I understand what you are saying and feeling. I've seen many countries in Europe, but none seem to offer the sense of freedom I think will be available here. Maybe it's just the newness, the virgin nature of everything, but I think there's something more. The open spaces, the uncluttered blue sky, abundant water—both fresh and salt—and the amazing animals and birds. Even the screech of the white cockatoos is music to my ears. You know, you can do your walks here just as readily as in Scotland, Joseph. For miles and miles and miles and miles, and almost always see something new around every bend. It's a great land.

"You mentioned the natives a minute ago. I plan to come out here more frequently in future as we invest more and more in the land. I meant to ask the overseer, but forgot. Have you had any trouble with the aborigines in the last two months, or is everything quiet?"

"Two of the three you travelled with up the Nepean, sir, still hang around a bit although they disappear for days at a time. We don't see Jack anymore. The others usually come for food and sometimes grog. I think their presence is good as the stories they take back to their tribes can only support our desire to be friendly with them all. At times I've seen smoke from small fires on the other side of the river so I presume they camp there. Too far away to see the actual people—maybe deliberate on their part. I've often wished I had time to explore the slopes over there to see if they've left any drawings in caves."

"Well, maybe when the crops are in you should go looking, Joseph. You'll have earned the time off. You do what you want to. Just make sure you bring in a good harvest so we can make some money down in the cities before you leave us. Now, I need to get back to the homestead, so I'll leave you here to check progress more closely. Good day and good luck to you." And with that Sir John was gone.

Joseph watched the man and his horse depart and rubbed his chin, deep in thought. "Yep, that's the man to a T. All chummy one minute but makes sure he lets you know you're beholden to him and have a job to do. Don't think we could ever be real mates. Makes me wonder if he'll ever have permanent friends, even in the upper class circles he relishes. Not for me to ever know, of course. Another month and I'll be off on my own farm. It'll be bye-bye, Sir John, thanks, and good luck to you."

Sir John's economic interests dictated many of his actions and were generally very successful. One couldn't always say the same for his politically oriented activities. Across the Nepean River at Emu Plains was a government penal establishment housing hundreds of chain gang convicts who were deployed to clear land, open and improve roads, and erect administrative buildings in the emerging towns in the extended geographical area. The men worked at hard labour ten or more hours per day. Punishment was severe and meted out far too readily, but the prisoners had little choice. Lashings were a daily occurrence, with few men spared the wrath of overzealous overseers. Recapture after an attempt to escape meant metered starvation, confinement in single cells baking in the sun, and whippings. Many a convict died from treatment there.

Especially when the crops needed harvesting, some of the better-behaved convicts were granted passes allowing them to work for free settlers in the vicinity, albeit for a very limited time period. These passes were a very special privilege which convicts longed for, as they provided a sense of freedom. Sir John was the beneficiary of much help of this form, yet, contrarily, a righteous aspect and hastiness in his make-up led to a particular error in judgment over camp activity that cost him dearly.

Early in the current year 1822 he blithely accused Governor Brisbane, the Colonial Secretary, and other high officials of sending convict women to the Emu Plains prison for prostitution purposes. An official inquiry could not substantiate his vindictive assertion and as a consequence, Sir John was *persona non grata* with the governor and the Colonial Office in London for some years to come. He was relieved of his magistracy in August, although it was to be restored under Governor Ralph Darling many years later in 1831. This was much to the chagrin of one of Governor Brisbane's close friends, who openly chastised Sir John in a verbose sour grapes diatribe in the *Sydney Monitor* newspaper in October of that year.

Because of his commitment to agriculture and the improvement of society, as recognized by successive governors, over time Sir John was the beneficiary of the largest assignment of convicts of any landowner. Between 1814 and 1824 eighty-five convicts were assigned to him in a variety of capacities.

The record keeping on convicts by authorities was surprisingly well organized. Each prisoner was assigned a unique number and was primarily identified by name and the ship (along with its master) which he or she had arrived on. The individual's crime, sentence, place of trial, year of arrival, trade (if any) and a description covering age, height, complexion, colour of hair and eyes, plus any distinguishing marks, rounded out each record. Officials could quickly identify and retrieve any records of interest.

The area containing Regentville was called "Evan" after Evan Nepean, Under Secretary to the Home Department in London, who had had responsibility for organizing the transportation of First Fleet Convicts to New South Wales in 1786 and who had helped select officials for the voyage, including Governor Arthur

Phillip. The river flowing by Sir John's estate was also named in recognition of the Under Secretary's role.

Coincidentally, at almost the same time that the Nepean received its name, the Royal Navy discovered the mouth of the Hawkesbury River, named after Baron Hawkesbury, about thirty miles north of Sydney Cove. It took a subsequent three years before officials determined that the two water findings actually matched and realized that two distinct names had been given to the same river. The names are preserved today, although applied in different sections of the river's course.

Convict records invariably included the name of the ships on which convicts arrived, and rolls were organized by ship name, rather than by the convict's name, or place of conviction, or trial date, all of which were secondary to record storage and retrieval. A Ticket of Leave was a document given to convicts when granting them freedom to work and live within a given district of the colony before their sentence expired or they were pardoned. Ticket of Leave convicts could hire themselves out (rather than be managed by the crown) or be self-employed. They could also acquire property. Church attendance was compulsory, as was appearing before a magistrate when required. Permission was needed before moving to another district, and 'passports' were issued to those convicts such as wagon drivers whose work required regular travel between districts. Convicts applied through their masters to the Bench Magistrates for a Ticket of Leave, and needed to have served a stipulated portion of their sentence.

Those sentenced to seven-year terms needed four years of service if all were spent with one master, five years under two masters. The analogous numbers for those with fourteen-year sentences were six and eight years, or twelve years under three masters. For lifers, eight years were required if only one master, ten years if two, and twelve if three.

Joseph had received his Ticket of Leave in 1819 and had plans to establish his own farm and farmhouse in the vicinity before his family arrived. Many convicts had similar aspirations, even those that didn't have families back home. They all hoped to find a loving, supportive wife and create a home of freedom in the new land.

5. Transition from Town to Country

Several years after the route across the mountains had been forged in 1813, Governor Macquarie urged the construction of a road from Sydney to Penrith. Sixteen sandstone markers indicated the mileage to both towns and these became the guidelines for everyone progressing west. In the early days of its existence the road was a major symbol of progress. Its point of departure was George Street and Sydney Cove, the genesis of the colony. Its route went west to Parramatta. Beyond, its symbolic character became more apparent, as the topography of long parallel ridges dipping down to the Nepean in prelude to the ascent of the great ramparts of the Blue Mountains on the other side of the river began to unfold. The road held a strange sense of promise to its travellers, a sense of anticipation quite unlike that felt on any other road out of Sydney.

In 1814, a stage cart service was established along Parramatta Road. Fares were ten shillings for passengers and three pence for letters. The colony's first stagecoach, valued at three hundred pounds, was imported in 1821 but did not begin regular service until 1823. The stage left the city at 7:00 a.m., arrived in Parramatta at 9:30 a.m., and left Parramatta for the return journey at 4:00 p.m. Inside passengers were charged six shillings. Hazards on the road included aborigines and bushrangers. In 1817 it was announced that all tree stumps would be removed and the road paved with stone, which would be covered with earth and gravel. A toll was levied on travellers who frequented the roadway. As usage grew, hotels and settlements sprang up along the way.

Soon after the First Fleet had arrived, Governor Arthur Phillip built a small hut for himself at Parramatta, as it became the administrative headquarters for government efforts and control outside Sydney. In 1799 this house was replaced by a larger residence which was substantially improved by Governor Lachlan Macquarie from 1815 to 1818, and which was used as a retreat by multiple governors until the 1850s, with Governor Brisbane making it his principal home for a short period in the 1820s. Sir John and the governor would often meet here, until their relationship deteriorated. The mansion survives today as Australia's oldest public building.

The selection of Parramatta for an official government presence did wonders for its economy. "Nalawa Daruganora," or "Sit down on Dharug land," the traditional greeting in the language of the local Dharug people, quickly gave way to white man's English, although in 1814 The 'Native Institution' school for aborigines was founded. The aborigines called the place Baramada, meaning "the place where the eels lie down." Eels and other sea creatures were attracted to nutrients created by the saltwater of Port Jackson meeting the freshwater of the Parramatta River. The river was not navigable beyond this point. In 1789 a convict named James Ruse was granted land for an experimental farm nearby on the condition that he develop a viable agriculture that could be emulated more broadly. There, Ruse became the first person to successfully grow grain in Australia. The Parramatta area in the 1790s was also the site of John Macarthur's farm where he pioneered the Australian wool industry.

A parsonage was built in 1816, and the Colonial Hospital erected in 1818. Military barracks were completed in 1820, as was St. John's Anglican Church. A year later the first Methodist church was built.

Initially in the penal colony, convict women were assigned as hut keepers to work gangs. Their position was perilous and many left and cohabited with male convicts to ensure a decent preservation. By the late 1790s 'women's huts' had been built in Parramatta, one of which was located on the north bank of the river where Parramatta's first gaol was built in 1796. In early 1804 weaving looms were established at the site with master weaver George Mealmaker appointed to oversee operations. The weaving establishment was known as the "Factory above the Gaol" and it was here in two upper rooms, each measuring eighty feet by twenty, that convict women worked and slept among the bales of wool. Overcrowding became a problem with up to two hundred women crammed into rooms meant for sixty.

The improved road from Sydney to Parramatta and, later, on to Penrith, made transport of goods from the Sydney docks to Regentville easier, and Sir John established his own fleet of horses, bullocks, drays, and wagons to move his supplies. It was recognized that the building of Sir John's Regentville home would take a long time, especially since many of his requirements would have to be imported from overseas. Marble was not yet sourced in Australia, foundries could not produce the sophisticated machinery he wanted, and the few local factories were not yet turning out fine pieces of furniture.

One aspect of building that was not an impediment to progress was the availability of craftsmen, for the convictions of men in Britain were not affected or influenced by whatever trade or industry they may have been employed in. Craftsmen were certainly available, one just had to find them—which is why Sir John kept up relationships wherever possible with officials managing the assignments of arriving convicts. Throughout 1822 and 1823 he accepted convicts from nearly all the arriving ships, especially craftsmen or 'mechanics' who could help with building his new abode. Some less talented convicts were kept in Sydney, however, as he proposed to move existing servants who knew his needs and habits to Regentville and consequently needed to train others to take their place in Sydney. It was a time to 'clean house' so he also let go a number of servants whose Tickets of Leave had been granted as well as those whose attitudes displeased him. It was a busy period.

By this time he'd also become bored with Catharine, who was listed as his 'housekeeper' in the 1823 musters. As mistress and mother of four-year-old Harriet she was allowed to stay on in Sydney, looking after the child, but was no longer in favour. At the grand balls at his mansion, and in other social events, Sir John was surrounded by beautiful women, many married, many single, many vying for his attention. Generous bosoms and cleavage proudly displayed in dresses of the times were a tantalizing part of the glamour of occasions evoking British traditions. Seduction in Victorian times was usually carried out quite discreetly and Sir John had his choice of female partners. He clearly enjoyed the opportunities for intimate liaisons that were proffered, and was arrogant enough not to worry about the decorum of discretion, nor the formality of marriage. As magnanimous and astute as he was in multiple facets of life, Sir John was not well disciplined in the art of keeping his trousers buttoned. He was an attractive man, in countenance, stature, wealth, intelligence, and social position, and many a woman offered him seductive delights.

Officers of the times were permitted to have mistresses as long as they didn't try to bring them into polite society. John didn't see any need to have just one mistress. He needed a housekeeper at the old house at Regentville where he now spent most of his time while building the new mansion. To that end he chose a twenty-three-year-old free spirit named Mary. Not just any Mary but one born in the colony, albeit to a female convict and a military man. Mary was none other than Mary Griffiths, daughter of Sir John's father's Norfolk Island friend, the marine, John Griffiths, and partner, Jane Thompson. Exemplifying his generosity, Sir John also hired Mary's father to work at Regentville as a dairyman.

Mary was a very attractive young woman, and given his natural proclivities, Sir John soon bedded her. She became housekeeper and mistress at Regentville in one fell swoop.

Once again Sir John had chosen a mate with a convict heritage, and had forsaken socially elegant and sophisticated young women of fine English backgrounds. All those perfumed bosoms now sagged in wonderment. Just who was this man?

6. *Regentville Design - 1823*

The Nepean River flowed northeast along the boundary of Sir John's property. From the river's southern edge the land rose gently to the east, and on the ridge nearly a mile from the bank, the architect Greenway and his men marked the foundation outlines for the new homestead. To maximize the long-range view of the river downstream the residence was designed to face north with a grand balcony across the front at the base of the second storey. The Blue Mountains rising on the opposite side of the river would provide early afternoon shadowing of the western sun, giving some protection from the vicious heat in summer.

The specific location along the river had been carefully chosen. In normal times and for most of its length along the property line the river was about one hundred feet across and generally ran fifteen to eighteen feet deep. But at one particular point a natural underwater upward sloping weir had formed, reducing the water depth to between four and five feet. Reinforced with large rocks and chips cut from the building blocks, a passable ford to the opposite bank became available for those on horseback, and the house was built to have ready access to it.

The underpinning of the extended Sydney region was sandstone, which ran in horizontal strata, providing an excellent base for huge city buildings in the years to come and yielding the primary material for the construction of Sir John's new home. West of the Nepean River the sand-stone strata had been forced upwards, extending from north to south, basically forming the range of hills known euphemistically in the colony as the Blue Mountains. It was not difficult to procure the needed material from the cliffs rising a mile beyond the opposite bank of the river

The main house was planned to be approximately eighty feet long by forty five feet deep, and two storeys tall. There were to be fifteen rooms, including the main public reception rooms and nine bedrooms. In the entry foyer a circular stone staircase was envisaged to be a grand showpiece. Across the front and on the two sides, a colonnade veranda was proposed with an iron balustrade bordering the balcony. Outside access to the balcony was via a staircase at the eastern end of the veranda.

By any measure this was to be an outstanding, imposing, elegant manor, rivaling anything built in Sydney, and indeed for that matter, homes of well-off families in many cities in England. Yet, in another sense the mansion was just a dot on the landscape of Sir John's extensive acreage at Regentville.

Francis Greenway pulled together a group of high-quality craftsmen and engineers. He started with workmen he had previously employed, and using Sir John's connections, added extra members from among the convict bands at the Hyde Park Barracks, in arriving ships, and in existing outland penal camps.

Thomas Badham hailed from Hereford. He was handed a fourteen-year sentence in 1817 at the Hereford Assizes and, along with two hundred other prisoners, was transported to Australia the following year on the *Tottenham*. He was a short, wiry fellow, red-faced, with beady hazel eyes and dark brown hair and a downcast disposition. But he was an excellent stone cutter and mason and in February 1822 started working for Sir John in Sydney. Late in 1823 at age twenty-six he was transferred to Regentville, where his unique skills were desperately needed, and he and a team of labourers built the walls of the great house.

As much as he was excellent at his work, Thomas was not a model prisoner by any measure. He would abscond twice, the second time in May 1826, after the mansion was completed. Even so, Sir John took him back to help build shelters at the stockyards. The stones were heavy, and the work breaking and shaping them hard. Years at the construction tasks would wear Thomas out prematurely and he would die at the young age of thirty-three.

The double front wooden doors of the house were centered and painted dark green, and to the east and west, three large vertical windows, almost the same size as the door frame, allowed the ground floor rooms to be well lit with natural light. Directly above were seven windows of the same size. Downstairs, the sunlight was filtered by the overhanging veranda at times.

Upstairs, there was no such protection and heavy drapes were planned to frame the windows inside.

Thomas worked hand in hand with John Day, a young but highly experienced carpenter. John had worked in the construction industry in London and had risen through the ranks of fellow workers because of his diligence, meticulousness, and pursuit of perfection. Admittedly he used more wood on some tasks than others, adding strength and intricate design embellishments which added costs, but the results made owners of buildings proud.

One evening back when he lived in London, John was out having a few drinks with his two friends, Thomas Edwards and Thomas Jacobs. Edwards was bored with life and craved more excitement. Playing cricket at the weekend just wasn't enough, and his accounting work was really very dull. On a whim he turned to his companions and said, "What say we go outside and have a little fun, chappies? How are your pickpocketing skills? Let's see how many men's kerchiefs we can bag in thirty minutes. What do you say? A challenge to liven up these nights which are all the same!"

Jacobs retorted: "Forget it, matey. Last thing we'd need would be to get nicked and put in gaol for something so trivial. Leave that to the poor 'uns who have to make a living that way."

"I'm in for a lark, Tom," rejoined John. "I'm tired of this pub anyway. Let's head for The Swan and see what we can manage along the way. After I finish m' ale of course."

"Arrrrgh, you two. I'll not be left here alone with this scurvy mob of drinkers. The Swan it is. But whoever scores a kerchief he can pawn buys the first round of beers there. Let me finish up."

Tipsy and laughing, the three staggered out of the Hounds and Hares and headed for the slightly upscale pub two streets over. One hundred yards short they stopped in a darkened doorway, waiting for a potential victim. A gent and his lady alighted from a carriage nearby, and two younger toffs, walking fast together, passed on the other side of the street.

"How long we gonna wait?" Jacobs whispered. "I gotta pee."

"So go round the corner, you weak ninny, or hold it," John replied. "We have to wait for just the right bloke."

Jacobs trotted off. Surprisingly he was back in no time excitedly waving a white embroidered kerchief that dimly reflected the poor lighting of a street lamp half a block away. "Look, I win," he triumphantly cried. "Here it is, mateys. I win, I win."

"Shush, you fool, how did you get it?" John demanded.

"Not fifty yards round the corner in an alley this gent was busy peeing at the base of a wall with both hands involved and his kerchief was stuck in his hatband. Like it was sitting up just begging to be taken. Couldn't pass up something so obvious, could I now? Even though I wanted to do what he was doing. Come on, let's check this linen piece inside the pub and see how good it is. And I've still gotta go. So hurry along. Who knows if he'll remember my face."

Edwards led them away quickly on a route designed to avoid any possible encounter with their victim. Their target was still The Swan so he chose a circuitous path that finally led them back to the front door. Most unfortunately, Mr. Oliver Green, kerchief owner, was inside describing to a constable his recent loss. Before Jacobs could do anything he'd been recognized and the constable was upon the three men in quick order. It wasn't a time to deny the police their due or to try and escape. Punishment would only be the more severe to fight the law, although many had tried and paid the price. Apparently their victim had gone to the pub not to search for his assailant but to mourn his loss, valued at two shillings. Day and Edwards were readily implicated as participants in the robbery scheme and receivers of stolen goods, especially since Day happened to have the kerchief in his possession on entering the pub. A sad ending for the lads on what should otherwise have been an ordinary day.

Each aged only nineteen, all three were found guilty in their trial on 17 April 1822 at Old Bailey, and sentenced to be transported for life. They were separated from one another in Middlesex gaol. Three months later John Day was placed on the five-hundred-ton convict ship *Eliza,* which left Sheerness on 20

July 1822, and arrived in Sydney four months later on 22 November. Fortunately, his trade stood him in good stead and he was soon released from Hyde Park barracks into the custody of Mr. Greenway. He quickly met up with Thomas Badham and they both worked on their benefactor's Sydney townhouse. By working together they avoided many pitfalls in the two subsequent years building the Regentville mansion.

Under Thomas' tutelage labourers carved and fitted the sandstone blocks for the main walls of the residence. As the walls grew in height John had his men create the framework necessary for floors and interior walls. Greenway was ever present ensuring his plans were precisely met.

Set back forty feet from the front line of the house, asymmetric wings were built on either side. The western wing, sixty feet in length and only one story tall, housed a large entertainment suite and a billiard room. Beyond the latter was a Greenway innovation in a gravity flushed multi-seat privy. The eastern one-storey wing contained the laundry and wash-house in front, bordering the slightly taller coach house which had a storage area above.

Between the wash-house and the back door, a steep flight of steps led down to a door that guarded the cellar where wine, fruit preserves, and vegetable roots were stored. Sir John imported fine wines from around the world, especially Europe, but the cellar also contained an extensive collection of wine made from his own vineyards.

The magnificent staircase that represented the opulence elsewhere rose to a large area upstairs from which halls ran north and south. Large closets for storage of towels and linens, and other decorative goods surrounded the central space and the halls led to bedrooms and two small bathrooms with sinks and baths. Italian marble had been deployed for counters and tiles and the bathrooms epitomized the elegance of a first class hotel. The attic above the second story held large containers for pumped river water, and two large upstairs fireplaces were used to heat cauldrons of water for hot baths. No luxury was spared.

Light had always been important to Sir John. Accordingly, some bedrooms had two windows, those for children one. Across both the front and back there were seven windows with four on each side. Adding to the modern design were two traditional dormers in the rear and one on each end. The mansion was incredibly attractive both inside and out.

From the back of the main house a covered way led to the servants' quarters and the adjoining kitchens and bakehouse. Sir John loved to entertain so the kitchens and bakehouse were huge, scaled at fifty feet by twenty feet, larger than many homes in Sydney. The servants' quarters were roughly thirty feet square and contained a servants' hall, or common room, plus seven bedrooms, six of which were dormer rooms within the roof space, three at the front, and three in the back. Designed for two people each, when compared to the main house bedroom sizes they clearly reflected the hierarchical social class distinctions of the time.

A small veranda at the back of the servants' quarters served as a communal meeting and relaxation place for all the employees.

Sir John had a passionate interest in horses. Some were necessary for transportation purposes but he also imported a number of thoroughbreds for racing. Consequently, at the back of the courtyard he had two stable houses built, holding a total of fourteen horses and harness rooms. Grooms and stable boys could sleep in overhead spaces. Between the two stable houses was a gateway, with separate cobblestone ramps leading directly into the buildings.

The complete set of buildings, from the main mansion to outbuildings and stables, formed the homestead complex and was surrounded with walls everywhere but the front. Gateways to the east and west complemented the one to the south. In all, the complex covered a site approximately one hundred ninety feet wide by two hundred feet deep, wider than a soccer field and two-thirds as long.

The size and design of the compound demanded special infrastructure support so Greenway sought engineers of varied backgrounds to help with plumbing, chimneys and fireplaces, reinforced stable design, laundry boilers, and kitchen fires and heat management. New water lines had to be laid from the pumping station, and its equipment upgraded. Sir John ordered the latest technology from England to offset the old machinery his father had put in place nearly fifteen years earlier.

Slowly, almost too slowly for Sir John's somewhat impatient liking, the mansion and accompanying buildings took shape. Delays in the expected arrival of machines, tools, and infrastructure supplies such as pipes were standard, as ships' schedules weren't known in advance, there being no communication back to the homeland except by ship-borne letter, which still took three months or more one way. There were times when Sir John's short fuse and abusive language made workers cringe, but since they had employment away from the chain gangs they suffered in silence.

Of an even more delicate nature were the requests for furnishings and service implements for the interior of the mansion. From beds to bedpans, from silverware to serving dishes, from drapes to quilts, saucepans to glasses, sheets to towels, tablecloths to serviettes, chairs to sofas, wine for the cellar, storage bins and wash pans, much had to be ordered from England to meet the level of quality Sir John demanded. There were of course local suppliers of soaps and candles and baskets and brooms and leather needs, and in some cases temporary Australian-manufactured goods were bought while waiting for better-quality English and European merchandise.

Not only did Sir John have fastidious taste, where possible his pride wanted to go one better than what the current landed aristocracy offered. One of the dinner services he ordered was designed specifically to his whims, being more ornate that anything found at a governor's residence. It was a Mason's dinner service in the Imari style characterized by broadly painted stylized images of foliage, flowers, and birds with geometric elements dividing the composition into panels: blue usually predominating, with red, green, orange, and sometimes yellow being used.

Jamison's pattern had extra gilding to detail the designs and border the coloured areas.

Mason's services were sold in standard sets of more than one hundred forty pieces, including large tureens and sauce tureens with stands, covered vegetable dishes, a salad bowl, a gravy dish, fifteen various sized serving dishes, some with drainers, two baking dishes, sixty dinner plates, twenty-four middle size plates, and bread plates.

Sir John was definitely preparing for large-scale entertaining.

As construction progressed the new mansion took on the name of the estate so that the title, 'Regentville', came to be used interchangeably for the house and the whole estate, as convenient. Its existence heralded the start of a new life for Sir John. His leadership in the agriculture industry, his patriotism, and his consequent support of democratic principles and man's freedom never changed, but the mansion gave him an elevated status socially in which he was rarely challenged. He could do whatever he wanted, to the extent that an almost hedonistic lifestyle emerged that added to his reputation and kept him in the public's eye for the following two decades.

7. *Regentville Construction - 1824*

Simon, the plaster craftsman, rolled up the canvas on the parquet floor, took one last look at the ceiling in the ballroom, smiled at the beautiful frescoes he'd created, and walked out the back door. Sir John was due at the weekend, and he was glad to be finished, because the man certainly could be a micromanaging task master. He didn't seem to understand that changes in temperature and the presence of heavy rains had a marked influence on what could and couldn't be done from a quality perspective. Simon retrieved the rest of his equipment and loaded up the dray. He walked around the main building and found Mr. Greenway, the architect, having a smoke on the front veranda, his horse tied to the veranda railing. A glass of lemonade sat on the small table beside him.

"Ah, Simon. All done?"

"Yes sir, finally. I must say it's been a delight creating such beautiful rooms. One doesn't always get the chance these days with everyone in a hurry to build. The end result makes up for all the changes imposed and the somewhat zealous supervision at times. I give Sir John credit for his taste. Any chance I could get a glass of lemonade? Sure is hot today."

"Certainly. Here, I haven't touched mine yet. Have this. I'll go get a second glass from Mary."

A plate of biscuits accompanied Francis' drink on his return, and the two men sat down on either side of the table. Simon took a large thirst-quenching gulp and chewed a frosted biscuit. "This is an incredible building. I've never worked on anything like it before. Modern, with all the latest devices, but still preserving some of the traditional aspects of a fine English manor. Nothing but the highest quality materials. It must be a pleasure for you to manage all this."

"Yes and no, Simon. As you have experienced, some of Sir John's requests are highly unusual and it takes a lot of effort to make them come to reality. I'm not only supervising the building work but also ordering and arranging all the household supplies that will make the place livable. Sir John has some decidedly singular interests. Only the best as you say, no matter what country it comes from, or what price. For example, some of the polished wooden tables were cut and fabricated a year ago in America especially for Sir John. And just this morning we had a problem with the new pumps bringing water from the river to the house and the orchards. We finally got the problem solved without having to order any extra parts, so that, among other things, it means the fountain out there in front of us will be playing when his Lordship arrives in two days' time. The statue on top is another very special art piece ordered from Italy."

"Well, I know it's taken a long time making it all happen, but it truly is an unbelievable place way out here in the country. Just how much land does the master own out here, Mr. Greenway?"

"Around the house and related service buildings here there'll be six hundred acres of gardens and parklands, so the mansion, per Sir John's words, 'will be like a lone sentinel in the middle of a beautiful park.' There's about two hundred acres beyond that where the crops are already growing, and where the orchards and grapevines are. In total there are over four thousand acres here. The labourers have already fenced off an enormous number of paddocks for merino sheep and Durham cattle plus a lesser number for pigs and goats, and of course pasture for all the horses. There are a number of chicken houses, and ponds and sheds for ducks, and lawns and huts for geese."

"My gosh I had no idea the estate was so extensive. How incredible!"

"Mind you, that's just here at Regentville. Sir John owns a number of other properties as well. On his last visit he proudly showed me that in all he owned just under five thousand freehold acres plus numerous grazing leases across the countryside. I have no doubt he's the wealthiest man in the colony at the moment.

"Another aspect that takes a lot of work is looking after all the labourers. You happen to be one who has earned his freedom and congratulations to you. There are two overseers managing all the convicts at the moment. You can probably imagine the effort required to keep everything looking beautiful in the parkland, as well as the number of men required to manage the crops and plantations, as well as all the livestock. Then there's the engineers who maintain the steam engines to drive the pumps for irrigation and the house water supply and the laundry boilers, and other labourers who look after all the farm machinery and tools. Thank heavens the overseers have some hard-working talented men under them who manage the different sections. Oh, and of course there are maids and servants that manage the household, and stable boys and a farrier. And a butcher. Somewhere inside in my little corner office I have a number of lists. I work with the overseers to manage the craftsmen and others working on the house here, but there are many more I don't see every day. I'm sure I'm forgetting some."

"You're exhausting me, Mr. Greenway, just listening to all the components of this place. I guess it's far more than a simple farm. Much, much more. Amazing!"

"There are plans for even more buildings and features. We already have over fifty convicts assigned to Sir John here. You've only seen the ones working around the house and maybe some you pass by coming to and fro. Once the furniture is in and the family moves in for good we'll need even more help. You probably aren't aware that a mile and a half down the road towards Mulgoa there's a camp with huts for all those convicts. We're going to have to build more huts soon. They have their own recreation area there as well—a big field where they can play football or cricket. I wouldn't be surprised when he visits this weekend if he comes with even more innovative ideas for the place. Of course he has the money to bring them to life.

"So saying, Simon, now that I've had a quick break, I need to go check how the chaps are coming along adding rocks to the river bed at the ford and finishing the boat house nearby. The land runs along the river in total for two and half miles. Make sure you leave your final invoice with Mary inside, and thank you for your work. I know Sir John will be pleased."

"Thank you. If I might ask, a reference from Sir John would certainly be a kindness that I'm sure would benefit my future business."

"I'll see what I can arrange for you. It shouldn't be a problem, so watch the post. Goodbye for now, and best wishes."

The men shook hands, and Francis picked up his hat, mounted his horse, and headed to the river.

Simon had his invoice neatly written out in anticipation of completion and hastened to the old residence to find the housekeeper Mary, whom he'd met months ago when first assigned to work on the new house. He was surprised to find her heavy with child, suffering somewhat in the heat of early March. She was charmingly gracious and indicated she'd pass his bill on to Sir John. Simon doffed his hat, wished her luck with the pending birth, and went on his way.

Two months later, on 16 May, Mary delivered a daughter, Jane Rebecca, named after her mother Jane Thompson, and possibly after Sir John's mother or first child who had died seven years before. Jane was the first of six children Sir John and Mary were to bring into the protected world of Regentville.

Sir John was incredibly proud of his mansion and enjoyed showing it off to anyone who expressed interest. William Horton, who worked for the Wesleyan Missionary Society, visited the house before its construction had been completed. In a diary entry dated 5 June 1824, he had the following to say:

"Sir John Jamison who resides on his estate opposite Emu Plains took me to see his new house. It stands on the top of a long gentle ascent and is certainly a noble mansion. It is seventy eight feet long by forty five wide, two stories high with a spacious cellar beneath. Each of the wings is fifty feet long. The outbuildings are detached and the whole premises will occupy about an acre of ground which is to be enclosed by a wall 14 feet high. It is built of fine durable stone and commands a very extensive and diversified prospect."

The cellar was a vital storage component of the villa. It had a root section and plenty of room for wines and spirits. Sir John had invested early in planting grapes for wine-making. Initially his cellar was full of fine imported wines of established French, Spanish, and Italian varieties. The wines from South Africa did not have the excellence of taste that those from Europe offered, nor did the efforts coming forth from Van Diemen's Land. For his own table only European wines were served, but bottles from the other countries were offered as gifts to visitors where appropriate. The difficulty of obtaining reliable supplies had led him to try and develop vines on his own estate. They were never as successful as he had hoped.

8. Unbecoming Behavior and Societal Progress

Back in Sydney, Sir John was having trouble with his trousers again. Attractive women, well encouraged, flirted with him openly. Catharine, the mother of his daughters, no longer in favour of his attentions, became a dressmaker, and started looking around for a more comforting companionship. In time she moved in with a James Wild, although not before producing another Sir John offspring, Thomas (Jamison) Cain. Harriet stayed at the Sydney house, while Thomas moved with Catharine.

Needing adoration and affection in Sydney as much as at Regentville, by mid-1824—shortly after the birth of Jane Rebecca at Regentville—Sir John took up with a new servant in Sydney named Elizabeth. Like his other mistresses Elizabeth came from a convict background. Born locally, she loved recounting the story of how she came to be.

Back in the old country her mother, Ann Long, had been born in the slums of London, about the same time that Captain Cook was discovering the eastern coast of Australia, although that meant nothing in her neighbourhood. She'd had a torrid life starting as a teen working the streets, eking out a miserable existence in the time-honoured profession. When one fleeting, minuscule chance to better herself was offered by a sympathetic patron Ann had grabbed it with all her might, never hesitating for an instant. Painstakingly, with dogged determination and grit, over ten years she gradually pulled herself up by her boot straps, successfully avoiding further prostitution. She worked hard at menial jobs, always giving more than asked, and was fortunate eventually to be chosen to participate in a small church experiment teaching the poor to read and write and learn the scriptures. She was more intelligent than many of her peers and from her early occupation had the added advantage of being street smart as well. As such, she could easily have joined the forces of successful con men and women taking advantage of others in the back alleys of the city. But she wanted to be better. Through her church connections, she finally secured a job as a maid serving the family of a church member who owned a small house in the West End. Ann stayed with the family until two years before the century ended when the gentleman owner was transferred to Edinburgh. Maids were already in place at the house he was assigned, so her employment ceased.

Even with a good reference in hand similar jobs were not easy to find as the city became flooded with displaced rural workers all looking for jobs and willing to be paid less. With her accumulated savings Ann was forced to rent a room at No. 20 Shipyard, and search more widely for a new position. Others boarding at the same establishment were also desperate, and some had reverted to stealing food or items to pawn in order to buy food. With savings running low Ann scrounged delivery jobs wherever she could, but also started stealing on very rare occasions and immediately pawning the items so plundered in order not to be caught with them in her possession. The one thing she vowed to herself was that no matter how bad things might become she would never retreat to serving men's needs again as she once had, no matter the potential money intake.

On Saturday 21 November 1801 she delivered a bunch of apples from Mrs. Roache's shop to Mr. Peacock's house in Chancery Lane. James Ross, servant to Mr. Peacock, took the apples upstairs to his master and returned with one shilling and sixpence for Ann. Later that afternoon Mr. Ross discovered a silver pint mug was missing from the sideboard in the dining parlour, and realized that the delivery woman had had easy access to it while he went upstairs. Indeed, Ann had pawned the mug at her favorite pawnbroker at six thirty that evening, which was where the constabulary found it two days later.

At her arrest she berated herself. "Why oh why did I let temptation in again? Because the pickings were so tempting, and so easy! Another small moment of weakness, but this time I will pay dearly for it. I should have used a different pawnbroker where I wasn't known. Oh dear."

On 2 December in her trial at Old Bailey, Ann Long was found guilty of stealing to the value of thirty-nine shillings, although the mug was worth far more, and sentenced to transportation for seven years. She spent the following nine months in the Middlesex gaol in horrible conditions before being placed with four hundred other convicts on the *Glatton*, which left London 23 September 1802 and arrived in Sydney 1 Mar 1803.

Sent to work at the original 'Factory above the Gaol' in Parramatta, she patiently performed her tasks weaving the horrid uniforms assigned to convict chain gang members. She accepted her punishment as due, and in time received her 'Certificate of Emancipation,' a document stating that her sentence had been served. Free at last, she immediately left the Factory, intent on resurrecting the old desire of a better life that had been put on hold for seven years—albeit in a new land about which she still knew very little.

The penal colony, now at fifteen years old, was still rough and raw in many ways. She realized that a lone woman would have a hard time on her own and so she travelled to Sydney, where she felt more opportunity would exist. Once again she turned to the church, where she quickly found a military man who was lonely, and available. Joshua Allott had arrived on the *Earl Cornwallis* 12 June 1801, having left Portsmouth 18 November 1800. As a sergeant in the Royal New South Wales Corps he had travelled with his wife, Jean, on what seemed like a never-ending voyage. They were on the seas seven months with stops in Rio and the Cape of Good Hope. Starting out with one hundred ninety-three male and ninety-five female convicts, the journey was beset by illness. By the time they reached Sydney twenty-seven men and eight women had died of dysentery despite the best efforts of the ship's surgeon, John Dight, and the captain, James Tennant. In fact, the ship had been fitted out with new fumigating lamps calculated "to prevent destruction caused by candles and other lights, of the oxygen or vital principle of the air, which is so essential to animation." They did nothing to curb dysentery, however, and most unfortunately, in the middle of July, only a few weeks after arrival, Jean Allott died. To travel so far, taking such a long time, and then to have his spouse die before even acclimating to the new world, left Joshua devastated, depressed, and desperate. Only his job kept him sane, and he took solace in his work and in the attentions of different women who sympathized with his plight.

He and Ann Long had a common need—another to care for, but not necessarily via a permanent union. Cohabitation provided a sense of security for both, making it easier to forge a new future. Ann became pregnant and on 3 June 1808 at age thirty-nine gave birth to a daughter, whom she named Elizabeth after the mother of the family that had originally hired her back in London. Recognizing that her child-bearing years were close to ending, Ann rejoiced in being able to bring the little girl into the world, and doted on her as a symbol of the more rewarding life she aspired to.

Joshua moved on, taking up with an Elizabeth Murray from Edinburgh, Scotland. Life and times were uncertain for many then and Joshua's spirit was still tormented with grief and loneliness. His new companion bore him a son, Joshua Joseph Elliott/Allott, (spelt variously) in 1810. Fragility, uncertainty, instability, and varying assessments of what the future might hold led Elizabeth into strange relationships. On 7 August 1812, while still cohabiting with Joshua, she birthed another son who was tellingly baptised Dougal McKellar Allott. Two and a half years later on 21 March 1815 she married Dougal McKellar in Parramatta, and bore him three sons and two daughters over the following ten years.

Joshua's soul finally steadied and he married Mary Champion in 1817. He lived to the ripe old age of ninety-three while his third known partner, Elizabeth Murray, lived to age 87. Living so long in the early colony days suggested both had marvelous internal fortitude and iron constitutions.

Meanwhile, Elizabeth Long, the daughter of his second love, and a proud first-generation Australian, learned to read and write and grew into a blythe spirit with an ever-ready smile and a positive, engaging, carefree disposition. At age sixteen she applied for a servant position at Mr. Jamison's home off George St. Her good looks, vibrant personality, and innocent sexuality ensured that she was hired on the spot, her lack of experience being totally disregarded. As was his way, Sir John took it upon himself to be her teacher, success registering the first night she helped him undress and put his clothes away. She was a happy young filly in his bed and elsewhere, and loved telling the tale of how different her life was from that of her mother, although she clearly didn't know its cruel start.

Vivacious, and broadly curious, with the run of the household, Elizabeth got to meet and know many employees—not only those in the serving capacity, but vendors and suppliers as well, plus some of the tradesmen working nearby on the next two houses for Sir John. Youthful and exuberant with a less-than-innocent flirtatious style, she became a figure of lust for many of the males around. While Sir John's pants went up and down with her help, he became resentful of the constant, sometimes embarrassing attention Elizabeth commanded around others. When he found she had also been intimate with one of the workers it was sufficient justification to dismiss her, unaware that she was pregnant, courtesy of his activities. The guidelines for his behaviour did not apply to others. In his mind he likened her to Henry VIII's wayward fifth wife, Catherine Howard.

John Ower had arrived in the colony with one hundred forty-five other prisoners on the *Mariner* 11 October 1816, having been convicted a year earlier on 30 September 1815 at the Perth Court of Justiciary. As a stonemason he was sent to help build the lighthouse on South Head, and for his good work there he was subsequently made overseer of stonemasons at Parramatta, where many government buildings were being commissioned. It was Francis Greenway who lured him back to Sydney to help construct Sir John's rental properties, and inadvertently to become overly friendly with Elizabeth.

Shortly after Elizabeth was removed from the Jamison home, she and Ower were secretly married way out of town at the Castlereagh Church on 13 April 1825. The couple moved to Liverpool, where a son, John Thomas, was born 12 August. When the baby was baptised in St. John's Church of England ten miles northeast in Parramatta on 11 September, the parents were recorded as Sir John Jameison [sic] and Elizabeth Ower, clearly reflecting Elizabeth's primary conquest and intimate relationship with Sir John.

No other children were born to John and Elizabeth, but young John became seriously ill in subsequent years and eventually died 7 April 1833 at age forty. Ever the opportunist, Elizabeth had been well prepared and not seven weeks later on 27 May at age twenty-five she married John Burgess at St. Luke's Church of England in Liverpool. Her son, jealously coddled and nurtured, was both her security blanket and revenge for being dismissed. He stayed with his mother throughout her life, before succumbing in 1878 at Liverpool.

Sir John had other passions beyond seducing attractive women. Eating fine food was one. He'd already exhibited another, racing horses, but was about to take that to a new level. The stables at Regentville could hold fourteen horses. There were special exits from the stables to the fields beyond, so that the horses never had to pass through any of the three main gates of the compound, coincidentally never impeding use of the gates by servants, tradesmen, and others. With his wealth, Sir John was able to import high-quality bloodstock from England and other countries. He employed a special cadre of horsemen including two dedicated groomsmen, James Hackett, and a youngster, Henry Richardson; a harness maker, James Eddowes; a farrier, John Taylor; a horse breaker, John Noble; and even his own blacksmith, Michael McCanna. All of these men, save for Henry Richardson who was born in the colony, were convicts with sentences ranging from seven years to life. Once again, a man's crime in a country far away was of little consequence if he possessed the skills and experience Sir John needed at any given time and place.

On 18 March 1825 Sir John convened a meeting in Sydney where a group of men founded The Sydney Turf Club. Sir John was elected President, while William Balcombe, Colonial Secretary, became Secretary and George Mills, Registrar of the Supreme Court, became Treasurer. Other founding members included

Thomas Kirkwood; John Mackaness, Sheriff of the colony; John Piper; Henry Thornton; William Wentworth; and Governor Brisbane, patron. Fees for membership and annual subscription were set to be payable in "Holey" Spanish dollars, even though the currency was under transformation.

When the colony was first founded, it ran into a problem with lack of coinage. Foreign coins—including British, Dutch, Indian, and Portuguese—were common in the early years, but much of this coin left the colony by way of trade with visiting merchant ships. The issue persisted for over twenty-five years until Governor Lachlan Macquarie conceived a solution when the British government sent out forty thousand Spanish dollars in 1812 for trade purposes. The governor hired a convicted forger named William Henshall to cut the centres out of the coins and counter-stamp these middles. The central plug became known as a 'dump' and was valued at fifteen English pence. It was restruck with a new design having a crown on the obverse, and the denomination, 'Fifteen Pence', on the reverse. Simultaneously the holey dollar received an overstamp, 'New South Wales 1813' around the hole on the obverse, and 'Five Shillings', equal to sixty pence, on the reverse. This distinguished the coins as belonging to the colony of New South Wales, creating the first official currency produced specifically for circulation there. Together the value of the 'dump' and the 'holey dollar' was twenty-five percent more than the value of a Spanish dollar, making it unprofitable to export the coins from the colony.

After wastage in the conversion process, which took a year, 39,910 holey dollars and 39,910 dumps were made. They were officially put into circulation in 1814. But as the wool, wheat, and coal trade with Britain increased and dominated exports, a cry for the use of British currency locally grew and in 1822 the government began to recall the coins and replace them with sterling coinage. The replacement took seven years before the holey dollar was demonetized, and the returned coins melted into bullion. Careful calculations at the time suggested that only three hundred fifty holey dollars and one thousand five hundred dumps remained. Some were lost, but many were hoarded as unique reminders of a short-lived currency. The value of even less-than-perfect examples rose dramatically over subsequent years.

The Sydney Turf Club evolved into the Australian Racing and Jockey Club in 1828, at which point Sir John gave up his presidency. By then, interest in horse racing was growing rapidly outside the Sydney environs and he helped establish the Hawkesbury Racing Club in 1829, of which he became patron. A few years later he built a racecourse in nearby Penrith, more convenient to his country estate.

Incredibly proud of his property, Sir John loved showing it off. He knew every crook and cranny of his mansion to the point that in listening to him espouse the details to fine degree many thought he had designed the place himself. Baron de Bougainville, the French circumnavigator of the world, included a firsthand description in his memoirs. He visited the new house on 6 August 1825 and commented as follows:

"Sir John, who is his own architect, makes us go over the smallest recesses of it. The house is of freestone and solidly constructed to a fairly attractive plan. The woodwork is in local cedar of a beautiful red-brown colour… When the mansion has been examined in all its aspects, and the decision taken, according to our advice, to change the main entrance of the [servant] apartments, we continue our walk in the direction of a beautiful valley, of which one part of the land is under exploitation; the rest, denuded of trees, except for the trunks, and enclosed by fences, serves as pasture for the herds."

Despite the praise, Sir John also had certain problems to contend with. The incredible size of the estate made it difficult to watch every part of it. For rascals and other less honest men it was a tempting target, so that thefts of sheep and cattle were not uncommon. Not only were animals removed but fence posts, wiring, and tools were also stolen. Sir John pursued criminals with vigour, and the thieves, if known, were often described in detail in the Principal Superintendent's column in the *Sydney Gazette and New South Wales Advertiser*. Descriptions to help identification such as, "ploughman, 5ft 5in, hazel eyes, dark brown hair, forehead bald, ruddy complexion" were taken from the ships' rolls on which prisoners arrived. Capture usually involved severe punishment. If a robber had escaped from a chain gang, he was sent back. He well and truly rued the day he had first thought of escaping, for the floggings on return were more contrived and relentless as cruel guards, semi-prisoners in their own way, not only were determined to deter escapist behaviour, but relieved their frustrations at not being able to escape their own plights.

There were great dichotomies in the convict world. Chain gang members toiled at hard labour twelve or more hours a day clearing land, or constructing roads, bridges, causeways, and public facilities for the benefit of the free. Punishment could be severe, and was often inhuman. At best there were fines and cautions, but too often even small indiscretions could result in floggings or sentences to the cells, treadmill, or public stocks.

Across the river from Regentville stood the Emu Plains convict camp where men worked on clearing fields up and down the Nepean and improving the main roadway over the Blue Mountains. Many were scarred physically and mentally for life, unfit to take on a normal life when their sentences concluded. At Regentville, a minimal number of overseers like Edward Walsh, and Patrick Mitchell, who was sixty years old, watched over their charges more for motivational and productivity purposes than from a punishment aspect. Floggings were very rare and only for gross misconduct. Problem convicts were more likely to be simply dismissed or left to be dealt with by the constabulary.

Compared to convict camps, life for convicts at Regentville was more of a reward than a trial.

9. Unpredictable Events

Sir John kept expanding his holdings at Regentville and by 1826, after purchasing Simeon Lord's 2,170-acre property named Frogmore, he had accumulated just under ten thousand freehold acres. He held a number of grazing leases as well, including one seven-hundred acreage named Cow-de-Knaves near Cabramatta and another grazing farm on Dog Trap Road. This road was lined with dingo traps and later the Cabramatta area became the scene of regular Hunt Club events in which the native dingo was substituted for the fox as the Huntsman's quarry. Sir John was an enthusiastic participant in such chases.

By colonial standards of the time Sir John's domestic arrangements were highly unconventional. This did not prevent him from mixing in the highest social circles, however. John Macarthur noted that Sir John openly kept two women (Mary Griffith and Elizabeth Long/Owen) and some years later Archdeacon Broughton found him "living in a state of 'concubinage' having children by more than one female." Sir John's arrogance in this regard was tolerated because of his wealth, entrepreneurial capabilities, support for the rights of his fellow man, and contributions to the country's progress.

When Lieutenant-General Sir Ralph Darling succeeded Sir Thomas Brisbane as Governor in December 1825 Sir John made haste to make his acquaintance. Over the six years of his term Darling would not be well appreciated by most of the citizens, as he was seen as a tyrannical ruler, banning certain social entertainment, and was accused of torturing prisoners. Among his recognized achievements, however, were the establishment of Van Diemen's Land as a separate political state with its own government, and initiation in 1826 of the convict-built Great Northern Road, linking the Hawkesbury settlements more directly with those in the Hunter Valley. The political capabilities of Sir John triumphed over any negative feelings and later he became an avid supporter of the governor, reaping judicial recognition and personal benefits.

That same year turned out to be the first of a prolonged drought, and Sir John was active, through the Agricultural Society, in working with Governor Darling to ensure new rules protected the public from illicit sales of dead cattle by ensuring slaughterhouses were licensed, and that contractors of turnpike gates kept a register of the number of animals passing through in order to prevent cattle stealing and killing. He also helped guarantee that supplies of beef, mutton, and other meat to the government commissariats would be secured by arranging government support of longer-term contracts with graziers. Sir John of course benefitted personally from such new arrangements, as did numerous other farmers and entities.

While Sir John dealt magnanimously with the problems of the country he still had time for family life. On 17 September Mary Elizabeth Jamison Griffiths was born at the mansion and the staff happily helped care for the new arrival. It was not until the 31 May in the following year that Mary and her elder sister Jane Rebecca were baptised in the little Anglican Castlereagh Church by its first pastor, Henry Fulton. As was common with children born out of wedlock the church recorded the birth under the mother's maiden name. In some ways this was helpful in Sir John's case as there were other families with Jamison-like surnames which often caused confusion. The actions of one family in particular were often mistakenly assigned to Sir John, despite obvious differences. This occurred in verbal communication and even in written matters sent to the Colonial Office.

In 1792 John and Mary Jamieson arrived on the *Royal Admiral* as free settlers. John had a mixed career after arrival, starting as superintendent of convicts at Norfolk Island, then manager of commissary grain at Toongabbie, and then superintendent of government stock. He was a brusque Scot who testified against Governor Bligh for stealing cattle, and was fired for incompetence upon detailed follow-up examination. Governor Macquarie approved Jamieson's reinstatement in 1810 but in May 1813 dismissed him for "gross neglect of duty." Jamieson retired and by 1820 had settled on twelve hundred acres near Liverpool. His faithful wife Mary had borne him two sons—William in 1796 and

John in 1799. Baptismal records for this John were later adjusted, erroneously, to show Sir John (in England at the time) as the father. Clearly, confusion around the name John Jami(e)son started early in the colony.

In December 1826 an unusual incident occurred involving John Jamieson (not Jamison) junior, who had married Sophia Burgen the year before. Sophia was the daughter of convicts Sarah Tandy and William Burgan, spelt variously, the latter having arrived with the Third Fleet in 1791. In keeping with standard practices John junior had several convicts assigned to him on his farm south of Campbelltown. One of them, Henry Preston, who had arrived on the *Glory* 1 May 1818, was a shepherd. Two days before Christmas he had called at the homestead to collect his weekly rations, but neither he nor his dog returned to his digs, and a fellow shepherd raised the alarm.

A brief search yielded nothing. Foul play was feared and suspicion fell upon a group of local aborigines. Jamieson decided to take the matter into his own hands. He left home with two armed men, rode to Wollondilly, and rounded up ten aborigines: two men, three women, a girl, and four boys. He charged them with killing his servant and took them prisoner. He claimed that four of the children admitted that Preston had been murdered, but that the murderer had gone to Bong Bong after cutting up his victim and burying the dog.

Jamieson and his men headed for Bong Bong. On seeing them, the suspect, known as Hole-in-the-Book, and his 'gin,' or woman, attempted to flee. Hole-in-the-Book was captured and, when the charges were laid upon him and a rope was produced, he ran. Jamieson fired two shots and Hole-in-the-Book fell dead.

Returning home, Jamieson interrogated his aboriginal prisoners as to the whereabouts of Preston's body. He was told that Preston had been cut into pieces, roasted, and eaten. So was his dog. Bones and entrails were produced, and Jamieson was shown where the fire was built. Later, a surgeon would testify that the bones were a shin bone, a left collar bone, and the lower bone of an arm, all human.

On 6 January 1827, Henry Preston walked out of the bush, unharmed. He had gotten lost, wandering eighty miles from the station. In May, Jamieson was tried for the manslaughter of Hole-in-the-Book. The trial aroused public interest, partly because of the allegations of cannibalism, and partly out of surprise that Jamieson had been charged at all. Justice Stephen, in directions to the jury, said, "It should never be understood for a moment, that the natives are not equally under the protection of the laws with any of His Majesty's subjects in the colony." In any event, the jury returned an immediate verdict of Not Guilty by reason of justifiable homicide.

In this case it was clear from the outset that Sir John was not involved, although there were occasions later when visitors asked him about the 'cannibal incident' based on their hearing the name Jamieson. But other strange incidents bothered him. One month before his daughters were baptised, an article appeared in the April 27 issue of *The Monitor* as follows:

"A respectable elderly female, in Pitt Street, who deals extensively in linen drapery, received a letter written by authority of Sir John Jamison, to proceed immediately to RegentVille, to receive an order from the owner of that elegant mansion, for a complete replenishment of all his linen stock, from the damask window curtains which hang in the saloon, down to the coarse towelling of the waiters at table. When the said female arrived at the mansion of Sir John, she had the mortification to find that she had been made the victim of a hoax, as full of impertinence as it was of ill-nature; and the only compensation the worthy person received for her trouble and long journey was a most courteous and hospitable reception from the noble proprietor of RegentVille, who entering into her feelings, gave orders to his steward and butler to make the good lady as happy as a sumptuously furnished larder and cellar could possibly accomplish."

Clearly, not everyone loved Sir John and he was frequently the target of both direct and indirect strikes against his property and good name. Still, he resolutely carried on caring for his fellow citizens. About the same time it was reported in a March 23 edition of the *Colonial Times and Tasmanian Advertiser* that:

'Sir John Jamieson, the well-known Australian speculatist, has sent to England for the materials to erect a similar structure [bridge] over the River Hawkesbury, which we may venture to say is full as wide as the South Esk, at the place where it would be necessary to erect a bridge.'

The bridge didn't eventuate until many, many years later, well after Sir John had passed on. When he wasn't busy racing his horses, conferring with politicians and bureaucrats, managing the Agricultural Society, or writing letters to the Colonial office on aspects of policy, Sir John took time to enjoy his social status and his elegant home. In October, with characteristic impulsiveness, he decided it was time once again to entertain on a lavish scale and proceeded to plan a Grand Ball, designed to establish a new societal standard for such events. The occasion? His fiftieth birthday, silently unobserved the previous year.

10. Servant Selection

Captain Carnes maneuvered the *Neptune* away from its berth at The Downs on the Kent coast and aided by a favorable wind quickly entered the English Channel. It was five days before Christmas 1817, but few on board were looking forward to any religious or festive celebration ahead. In the under-deck, one hundred seventy male convicts jostled for position and space, bracing themselves using their backs against the stanchions as the four-hundred-seventy-seven-ton barque moved into the heavy swells. The vast majority of the men had never been on a ship before. Some had been incarcerated in prison hulks on the Thames but those rotting boats only rocked gently with the tide, causing little distress with their movement. No matter their background, all the men were destined to experience some form of sea-sickness within the first few days of being on the water.

William Shillito was no exception. Several months earlier at age twenty-five he'd been convicted of stealing from his employer where he'd been a sort of butler-come-handyman fulfilling a variety of functions. His punishment was meted out as seven years transportation. Like most on board he regretted his foolishness, but it was too late now. English society was getting rid of another load of depraved criminals who were receiving the justice they rightly deserved. "Out of sight, out of mind" was a prominent colloquial epitaph.

Unknowingly, the convicts on this boat were to fare far better on their journey than tens of thousands of others who made similar voyages in years both before and after. For on board happened to be Surgeon Superintendent Thomas Reid, one of the more professional, compassionate, and competent surgeons to serve His Majesty. The convicts were organized into 'messes,' six persons in each, one of whom was appointed to superintend the mess. This sub-division of duty among the men was calculated to inspire confidence in the measures to be adopted, and gave the temporary officers a considerable degree of authority among their companions. Each monitor served as a check upon the others, whilst the reactive watchfulness upon one another's actions produced a kind of rivalry amongst them in responding to commands.

Before the ship left the docks, Dr. Reid drew up and presented to the men a set of guidelines for behavior and discipline. He was pleasantly surprised to find that none of the men objected. Indeed some contrarily offered a grudging acknowledgment of their value. The six basic tenets were:

1. You are not to curse or swear, use obscene or filthy conversation, fight, quarrel, or steal from one another, use provoking words, or call any one but by his proper name.
2. You are to be respectful and obedient at all times to the officer and guards.
3. Cleanliness being essentially necessary to the health, comfort, and well-beingof every person on board, it is particularly desired that the strictest attention be paid to it on every occasion.
4. Those to whom the management and care of the messes may be entrusted, are desired to be careful in attending to their duties, as they will be held responsible, and, in case of failure, punished severely.
5. Any one refusing to obey the directions of those who have the charge of messes, etc. will, on being detected, receive such punishment as the circumstance may deserve. A faithful report will be made of every man's conduct; and those who behave well, though they may have come here with bad characters, will be favorably represented.
6. The prisoner that shall dare to break through the above rules will be punished in proportion to his offence; and any one so offending must never expect to be recommended to the notice of the Governor of New South Wales.

Copies of the guidelines were printed and placed in conspicuous places around the ship with the additional written threat that any man found defacing or destroying the rules would be punished severely. The heaviness of the latter proclamation was balanced by Reid's purchase and distribution of a number of bibles and prayer books for the convicts' use. As well, once the ship was under way, Reid sought out the twenty-three convicts less than twenty years old, one being only thirteen, and set up a school under the care of a convict appointed as schoolmaster. The school operated for the whole hundred and forty plus days of the voyage, at the end of which all the youngsters were literate. Providing appropriate discipline and keeping the convicts active not only limited them from dwelling too much on their past or the unknown future, but also provided healthy exercise. Reid insisted on enforcing cleanliness in every part of the ship, including the prison, by having the decks regularly scraped, scoured, and washed. The interior of the ship and prison was ventilated, or warmed by stoves as the occasion dictated.

The *Neptune* planned to stop at Capetown to effect a few small repairs resulting from heavy storms in the North Atlantic and to take on new supplies of food and water. On arrival Captain Carnes was informed, to his dismay, that sixteen extra prisoners were to be boarded. These men had escaped from Sydney by hiding in the hold of the *Harriet* for a month before being discovered almost at the point of starvation, and were being returned. Extra lodging capacity had to be built extending the prison and soldiers' quarters, thereby delaying departure. The new prisoners were kept separate from the other prisoners, being effectively excluded from the society and conversation of the original convicts. However, religious books were provided and they were allowed to bathe and exercise in the open air. They were not allowed any wine, but the 'old' prisoners requested permission to share their allowance of wine with the new prisoners, which Reid allowed. On arrival in Sydney 5 May 1818, the sixteen men, Henry Chambers, John Druet, Benjamin Oliver, John Cochrane, Robert Plummer, John Skelton, Patrick Lowry, Nathaniel Ewer, Henry Moore, William Hollady, John Latham, James Quinn, Benjamin Little, William Chapman, Thomas Edwards, and Moses Solomon (a boy), each received one hundred lashes and were forced to work on a chain gang for the following twelve months. Punishment was quite harsh for misbehaving convicts.

The most intriguing and unique aspect of the voyage, however, was that every one of the final one hundred eighty-six convicts on board signed a letter of thanks to the surgeon, Thomas

Reid, for his "unremitting attention and care" during the trip. This deed was an unprecedented recognition of a shipboard doctor's worth, and was never to be repeated.

William Shillito, the thief previously mentioned, was one of the men who willingly signed the document. He had seven years to serve at His Majesty's pleasure, and was fortunate to be assigned immediately as a servant to a merchant who owned warehouses along the waterfront in Parramatta.

William would carefully watch the arrival of female convicts who were brought up-river from Sydney. These primarily were women and girls who could not find assignment in Sydney as servants. In 1821, responding to overcrowding, a new facility for housing the women was built by convict labour on a four-acre site, from locally quarried sandstone, at a cost of 4,778 pounds sterling. It became known as 'The Female Factory', with the walls of the main building ranging from two feet six inches thick at the foundation to twenty inches at the apex of its three storeys. It had an oak shingled roof, floors of paving or string-bark six inches thick, with barred leadlight windows in the basement and lead glazed windows on the upper floors. The first floor was used for meals, with the top two floors for sleeping. The porter, deputy superintendent, superintendent, and matron were provided separate accommodations on the site.

The building was often referred to as the 'Old Stone Jug' and over time served as a refuge, a gaol, an asylum, a home for the infirm, a labor exchange, a marriage bureau, a hospital, and a factory. It was the site of the colony's first manufactured export, producing sixty thousand yards of woven cloth in 1822. Generally speaking, however, the women wove distinctive uniforms for convicts on chain gangs. Originally intended as a place of refuge for the women and children of the colony, within a decade it became more like a conventional prison with all the attendant problems of forced incarceration.

Mary Ann Hudson was born in Brighton in 1796, and moved to London at age twenty, where she found a position as cook to a middle class family. As the family grew larger, demands on her shopping and preparation time increased disproportionately. After more than seven years of service, tiring of what she felt were totally inconsiderate and unreasonable work hours, she said goodbye, determined to find a better job for herself.

Lack of meaningful interaction with the outside world, however, had left her with misconceptions about how easy it would be to find something new. She moved from abode to abode, renting rooms or sometimes just space, knocking on doors, scouring public notices and advertisements, looking for replacement employment. She'd saved money but now had to spend it on lodging and food, which she hadn't had to do before. It wasn't long before her meager funds were disappearing at an unhealthy rate while her despair was simultaneously increasing at a corresponding inverse rate. In February 1824 she found sleeping space in a room above a confectioner's shop owned by Ruth and John Bamber. One morning after lighting the fire in their bedroom she stole two boxes of money and clothes from the dresser and absconded. She was caught twelve days later and held in Middlesex gaol for trial, which occurred on 7 April 1824.

Since she still had some of the stolen clothes with her when caught, she had nothing to say in her defense and was convicted with a life sentence, to be served in Australia. She ended up as one of eighty-one female prisoners on the *Grenada,* which left London 2 October 1824. Well before sighting Tenerife the ship encountered a massive North Atlantic early winter storm and was hove-to for three days. The twenty-one cabin passengers were confined to their semi-comfortable rooms and the saloon. The conditions below deck for the women and the accompanying fifteen children, however, were almost unendurable. In heavy seas, hatches were always battened down, and every scuttle closed. No fresh air reached them at all for there was no deliberate ventilation of any kind. The stench was appalling. Nor was it possible for them to leave their close-set tiers of bunks. Each time a big wave crashed on the deck above, several tons of water flooded down, drenching bed sheets, mattresses, and clothes. Sometimes even exhausted sleepers were washed from their bunks. The elders among the passengers became grave and anxious, but young children, having gotten over their seasickness, thought it high fun to slide toboggan fashion, on a child's chair laid on its back, across the deck from side to side as the ship rolled. Weary parents were not amused, but too ill in most cases to effect discipline.

Most of the prisoners were petty thieves who had stolen something small to pawn in order to buy food. Some had stolen bigger artifacts, including Mary Ann, and there were a few who were much cruder—prostitutes of varying ages and others who had been caught after being involuntarily cut in knife fights in seedy pubs. No one could suggest that in aggregate they were a fair representation of the gentler sex, although they jokingly referred to themselves as "The Ladies." At one point a decidedly attractive young woman of warm temperament was detected in a passionate, vulgar flirtation with one of the crew. She was apprehended by the surgeon, who admonished her, whereupon she suddenly became violent with him verbally and physically. With help from soldiers she was brought on deck and spread-eagled, then lifted screaming and struggling on to the rail of the bulwark. Her extended legs and arms were bound to the main shrouds and she was left to rave and swear helplessly in the embarrassing position until she cooled down.

With no other marked incidents Captain Alexander Anderson brought the ship into Sydney Cove on 23 January 1825. They'd left London in late autumn with the weather cooling, and had arrived in the colony in the hottest part of summer. Two days spent in stifling conditions on board before being mustered didn't help the prisoners' dispositions. And most, instead of going ashore as hoped, were placed on smaller boats for transport to Parramatta. It was the day before Australia Day.

And thus it was that William Shillito happened to be standing on the dock the day Mary Hudson and twenty other young women were landed and marched to the Female Factory. She was just one of a crowd of no special distinction beyond having flaming red hair which reminded William of his younger sister. She'd never replied to the letters he had had scribed, although he'd written to her and his father several times. He reasoned that they'd never gotten over the shame of his crime. His only solace was that fellow convicts experienced similar abandonment. Late in the year William received his Certificate of Release, having served his time. This meant, to all intents and purposes, that he was a free man, entitled to own land and work for himself if he so chose. He was now superintendent of the warehouses, earning a nice little income, and he wasn't sure what he wanted to do next. In a way he didn't care much for Parramatta and the burgeoning town environment with all the attention by governors and other officials, and the increased military presence. With the pardon behind him he wondered if his new status might make marriage an attractive prospect for some pretty woman. He'd recently turned thirty-three, and while there'd been a few short-term satisfying liaisons over the last seven years he was more interested now in permanent companionship and even the possibility of raising a family.

The Female Factory was a logical source of potential mates and had provided many wives for men over the years. In fact, the practice was so common that a special process was available to interested suitors. In the first quarter of 1826 William arranged to obtain a certificate from a local magistrate which attested to the notion that he was an appropriate and 'proper' person to seek a wife from the Factory. By appointment he presented this to the matron and master of the institution. After the validity of the certificate had been checked, William was ushered to a special room in the building. The matron proceeded to the department which held the best-behaved women and indicated to them that a gentleman was present seeking a wife. She provided limited information about William and asked that anyone who would like to talk to him to step forward. Those interested were then marshaled in batches and led into William's presence.

It was a daunting experience to say the least to find so many women seeking marriage as an alternative to the Factory work. As the women entered the room William would approach those that caught his attention, inquiring of their age, family background, religion, crime, experience, and desires. Similar questions were raised of him in order to find common ground and outlook.

In general when such an opportunity arose in these managed meetings, of most importance to the women were the applicant's status; his holdings of cattle or sheep if free, and in any event, details of his job and previous family if any; his interest in children, and his financial position.

For William these interchanges proceeded for a good two hours until he found himself tiring. He asked the matron for a glass of water just as a smiling woman with orange locks entered. He recognized her immediately as the one he'd noticed arriving back in January a year ago. Memories of his sister stirred but he quickly brushed them aside, anxious to learn more about this attractive lady. She was a few years younger than he was but obviously more mature than many of the youthful girls he'd been talking to up to this point. Mary Ann's responses to his questions were most satisfying, and similar realizations emanated on her side as well. The ever-present and experienced matron, who had witnessed all types of interchanges over the years, quickly identified a high degree of mutual attraction and smiled to herself. Another good worker would be gone, but a replacement would soon be found to take her spot. And another single, lonely man would be made happy. What more could she ask for?

After further intense conversation between William and Mary Ann resulted in a joint commitment to marry, the matron helped set a wedding date for the pair and arranged completion of the marriage application. Within days Mary Ann was saying goodbye to her limited circle of envious friends as she left on William's arm, no longer clothed in convict 'slops' but wearing a pretty dress and bonnet. A new life awaited both of them.

Sadly, that new life was soon to face a non-trivial and highly annoying obstacle. One of the women who had fancied William through the interview process was highly miffed at being passed over and discarded in Mary Ann's wake. At Catholic mass on the Sunday following the managed exchanges she sought out the visiting priest and indicated she was aware of a great sin, wherein one of the less numerous Protestant flock of women at the Factory, who had left a husband behind in London, had recently presented herself as single in order to marry a local free man. In this slight misrepresentation she passed on no names in order to lessen her own duplicity, but the priest, bound to uphold his relationship with the prison, the magistrates, and even his competitive peers, passed the information on as an unsubstantiated rumour to his good friend the Protestant parson. Since only about twenty percent of the Factory inmates were Protestant it didn't take long for the minister to identify Mary as the wayward sinner. Duty bound, he checked with the Sydney church authorities, who then documented their refusal to approve the Hudson/Shillito marriage application on the basis that Mary was already married.

William was shocked at the news, for he and Mary had been cohabiting for a month while waiting for their marriage application to be approved, and were enjoying being together immensely. Mary Ann was likewise stunned, claiming the information was totally false. She and William made an appointment to talk to the pastor whose name was on the application, and to the magistrate who had informed them of the refusal of their application. Mary's story was sad but not unfamiliar. She had indeed been married at one time at age eighteen. Two years before that her aging parents had migrated to southern Spain, leaving her behind in the care of a maiden aunt who was only interested in the annual management stipend she received from the parents. Unloved, lonely, feeling abandoned, Mary married a local fisherman named Ian Cullen. For two years, although life was hard, she experienced a love and appreciation she'd not known previously. But misery returned when Ian drowned at sea in a violent storm. He was buried at St. Nicholas Church of England, at which time Mary decided the town had brought her nothing but grief and she headed for London, reverting to her maiden name, hoping to let the past fade in her memory. At her incarceration after her trial she mentioned she had been married earlier, and that record now stood in the way since her husband's death had not been noted.

The magistrate explained that since the marriage issue had been raised she must now arrange to get a copy of her ex-husband's death record from the church in Brighton, or from the civil authorities there, in order to prove her story and to have a new marriage application approved. Vexed, disappointed, and frustrated, Mary and William hired a solicitor to create the necessary paperwork and manage the process of contacting authorities back in Brighton to recover the appropriate information to prove her widowed state. Given the journey period of four months for the grand sailing ships of the times, it took nearly eighteen months from the time of the solicitor's initial inquiry and response from Brighton to final payment arrangements and receipt of a legal document.

Sir John's old magistracy connections led him to hear of the unusual case, and in one of his exemplary compassionate acts in late 1826 he offered the couple employment at Regentville. Mary Ann became his cook and William his butler. They shared one of the small rooms in the servants' quarters, and while they waited for paperwork, Jane Catherine Hudson Shillito arrived in the world 5 February 1827, and was baptized 18 August at Castlereagh Church. With evidence at last in hand William and Mary were finally married at St. John's Anglican Church in Parramatta 16 June 1828.

11. *Social Experiences*

Ann Kingswood, Judith Merriman, and Sarah Woolsley were thrilled when they received their formal invitations to the Regentville Ball. At last they had achieved the recognition that had eluded them for longer than they thought appropriate. But this was Australia, after all, not dear old refined England. Social customs and procedures were a little behind those they had been raised around back home.

In their early twenties, the girls had travelled to the colony accompanying their military parents on the same ship, the *Guilford*, arriving July 1822. Along the way they had found a number of common interests and desires, and a strong friendship had ensued. All were from London, but at different positions sibling-wise in their families. Sarah was the first of two daughters with an older brother and was the eldest of the threesome. She was studious and well educated with a quick wit and repartee, though perhaps a bit more reserved than her companions. Ann was a single child born late in life to older parents, each married previously with no other children. In part she'd been a nurturer and caretaker and had a loving disposition juxtaposed with a certain naiveté that her friends constantly found amusing. Judith was the youngest and most spirited of the trio. With two older brothers and a happy-go-lucky doting father, she was daring and creative. Her effervescent personality made her the centre of any gathering, and her infectious laugh readily drew people toward her.

"I am going to wear something bold and gold," Judith declared to Ann and Sarah at morning tea near the Quay, "because I understand Sir John loves that colour."

"Well, you'll need more than that to grab his attention, my dear," Ann responded. "I daresay you have the figure but you'll have to do something special with your hair. Your carrot top really stands out so it will be very noticeable."

"I might add a small tiara. While I seriously doubt that many (if any) other women will have the same coloured hair the combination may help me stand out even more, especially with a gold dress if I let the tresses fall on the gown at my shoulders."

"Sounds to me like you are planning a little flirting already," Sarah chimed in. "Am I right?"

"Well, just how many chances does one get to meet the wealthiest man in the colony? I wouldn't mind being in his favour. Are you not interested as well?"

"Definitely not," were the simultaneous responses. Ann added, "I'd be scared to be so close to someone as smart as him. I know very little about politics, or banking, or horse racing, so what would we talk about?"

With a mischievous smile Judith whispered, "I wasn't thinking of doing a lot of talking."

Shocked, Sarah whispered back, "Am I hearing you right, Judith, you are going to try and bed the good knight? You must be joking with us. Ann?"

"You can't be serious, Judith. What on earth makes you think he'd be interested, and why would you want to anyway? Just because you're not a virgin like Sarah and me doesn't mean you can...well, maybe it does, I don't know. But after all, he walks in the halls of high society and knows scores of well-to-do women. Surely his 'interests' would be directed to one of them more than you."

Ann's forehead creased in a frown but Judith's flashing eyes and huge smile made it clear that nothing the others could say would change the intentions building in her own mind and body.

Throwing up her hands and looking despairingly at Sarah, accepting the impossibility of having any impact on Judith's decision, Ann burst out laughing. "Judith, you are utterly incorrigible."

Sarah joined in but her natural reserve was dwelling on the 'hows' and consequences of Judith's intentions. "Why would he even give you a second glance, Judith? I don't understand—even with your dazzling figure, hair, and personality, you will be competing with more mature and experienced women."

"I haven't worked it all out yet, girls, but it will happen. Some things I do know. While he seems to prefer mistresses with convict blood in them, I understand he's nowhere near as particular with one-time encounters. He's also reputed to like younger women. Yes, there will be other younger debutantes there. So how can I be so different that he will want to spend time with me?" She thought for a moment, then said, "Here's an idea. What if I take him a gift?"

"Other guests will do that too, Judith. After all, it is a birthday celebration. Not all of them, but that won't be unique."

"But Ann, won't those gifts primarily be from menfolk or from couples per se? Cigars, a bottle of fine port, a small framed painting of Sydney Cove, an old pistol, and so on. What woman would offer something masculine?"

"You've posed exactly the appropriate question. What do you have in mind?"

"Well, on the occasion of their fiftieth wedding anniversary my grandfather gave my grandmother a beautiful heart-shaped locket made of pure gold. That locket now belongs to me. It is over an inch tall and nearly as wide, and has its own little gold key that opens it. Originally, inside, my grandfather had drawn a tiny ink picture of himself and my grandmother sitting side by side on a bench holding hands and looking at each other with adoring smiles. At least that's what I was told."

Ann commented, "So, you own a locket like many of us, although yours sounds much bigger than the one attached to my bracelet. What about you, Sarah?"

"Yes, I have one tucked away in my glory box. It belonged to my mother as a little girl. It was a gift from an aunt when she was baptised."

"Well, here's my plan. I will wear my locket at the base of my throat, and have the key placed in a small ring box which I will present to Sir John. I'll tell him how much of an admirer I am and that the box contains the key to my heart, but say nothing more. I'll have a flattering miniature ink drawing of him placed inside so that if he does become curious and wants to open the locket he'll see just how important he is. I'm sure it will be difficult for him not to want to know more about me. At least I will help make it so."

Sarah smiled and laughingly said, "You amaze me, Judith. You are so...bold and daring! Knowing you I would definitely not wager against your success. You are absolutely incredible, no doubt about it."

Ann backed her up. "Only you, Judith, would be brazen enough to plan such a scheme. Unbelievable! That's what you are. And, what's more, you will probably succeed. I can't wait to see if you really will do it. At the very least you deserve another cup of tea and a biscuit... Waiter!"

The line of carriages stretched from the front door all the way back through the parkland to the main entrance gates. When each coach came to a final stop at the house, a groom helped the occupants carefully disembark, then led the driver and empty conveyance to a field beyond the stables. The parade of arrivals included military officials in uniform, and politicians in evening wear with their beautifully dressed wives and girlfriends, young debutantes with specially chosen partners for the evening, ships' captains and surgeons in splendid uniforms, wealthy merchants, judges and other bureaucrats, and even a few select clergymen who had purposely left their clerical collars at home allowing their purple vests to indicate their status. The cream of society had been invited, with only a few souls declining the opportunity to see and be seen at Sir John's magnificent new residence. It was well known how magnificent his parties were, and grand balls were legendary.

On horseback came the local neighbouring well-to-do farmers dressed in their one and only suit, plus a friendly magistrate from the local courthouse, and the clerk from the Title office. The constabulary was present in a semi-official capacity—supposedly available in case of unwanted drunken behaviour or unnecessary fighting, but also invited to enjoy the festivities discreetly.

The entrance gates at roadside were decorated with ivy and baskets of fruits and special hanging lanterns. The mansion veranda was festive with decorative lights, and to one side were special amenities with a demure maid-in-waiting where visitors could brush off the dust of their ride and wash their hands clean, before entering the main foyer and greeting Sir John. The Knight of Regentville was in grand form. He loved parties, especially where he was the centre of attention. He was dressed in impeccable finery—a long lightweight maroon coat fell from his shoulders behind him as he stood at the base of the marble staircase; a silk blouse with pearl buttons at the wrist and down the front cleverly concealed a slight paunch; a soft yellow and blue cravat decorated his throat and a series of gold chain necklaces crossed his chest. His beard and moustache were elegantly trimmed and a hint of eau de cologne wafted forward. In his left hand he held partially open an elegant handkerchief, showing a substantial hemstitched border embroidered with blue ships. His large eyes sparkled with unfeigned pleasure and merriment, for he was thoroughly enjoying himself. His right hand was offered to gentlemen for a welcome greeting, but with ladies he took their gloved hand in his and lifted it to his lips where he bestowed a charming kiss. Many men nodded their heads in deference as they said good evening and some of the ladies offered a slight curtsy as if in the presence of royalty. Respect and admiration filled the entry foyer.

Coats and accessories were received by maids who took them upstairs to one of the several bedrooms allocated to the necessary temporary storage and keeping. Since it was mid-spring the number of coats and furs were limited but in themselves were a testament to the wealth of the prominent owners. Extra staff had been hired to help with the massive organization required to manage the event. Maids, groomsmen, waiters, cooks' helpers, and numerous others had been vetted and quickly trained to their specific functions, with most of the guests unaware that all but a handful of those serving them were convicts.

Sir John's shoemaker had created a unique pair of white leather shoes with blue laces, matching the colour in the cravat and on the handkerchief. Pure white pants with gold piping down the inside and outside legs were held up with an ivory-coloured leather belt adorned with a large gold buckle in front. The stream of white waistcoats, black silk breeches and black tailcoats passing by helped make Sir John's outfit stand out even more so than otherwise, competing more with the ladies' finery than anything else. And what finery they displayed. Seamstresses had been busy in Sydney and Parramatta for weeks, creating new designs, trying new combinations of lace and material to come up with something both unique and flattering to the wearer. In some instances colours were chosen to enhance the showing of large heirloom jewels such as emeralds and rubies. In other situations madam had scoured the local jewelry stores to find something to complement her new gown. The end result couldn't have pleased Sir John more as he delighted in admiring the seemingly endless parade of fine jewels bobbing between perfumed breasts. His eyes made no secret of his interest and many a lady's hand was held, and small talk sustained, far longer than expected.

In the huge ballroom, two bands in separate corners alternated throughout the evening and night in providing light music for dancing. The enormous room was decorated with framed pictures of Jamison ancestors, past kings and queens, and ships of the Royal Navy. For the occasion it was festooned with extra lighting and sparkling silver and gold pendants. A number of chairs and tables placed around the perimeter permitted small groups to converse while sitting although most visitors stood and watched the dancers twirling at the far end of the room. Champagne in special flutes was served by uniformed waiters and waitresses who moved gracefully between groups engaged in social dialogue. It was as if a scene out of an English mansion had been transported across the seas with everything intact. A little corner of old-world charm in the Australian bushland.

Shortly after 10:00 p.m. when all the guests had arrived, a substantial drum roll commanded everyone's attention as Sir John mounted a foot-high dais and welcomed his guests. Well over two hundred faces turned to smile at the host who then proposed a toast to His Majesty, followed by one to Governor Darling, and other important attendees in succession. Seemingly from nowhere a young man mounted the dais beside him and introduced himself as Thomas, Sir John's brother, and proposed a further special toast to honour of Sir John's birthday. The band struck up "For He's a Jolly Good Fellow" and the crowd enthusiastically sang and applauded their host's occasion. Stepping down, Sir John immediately asked the governor's wife for a dance and the music flowed on accordingly. The gaiety and noise returned as the party got officially under way. Sir John was a natural conversationalist and moved from group to group engaging in political debate, agricultural discussions, business propositions, or, most especially with the ladies, talk of the mansion, the decorations, social change, and even English and European fashion. No woman could resist his call to the dance floor and he spared no exertion in up-tempo swings and movements. Many a partner was returned to her seat aglow from the efforts of keeping up with him.

Many were surprised to learn about the young gentleman who had reminded everyone of the reason for the ball. Thomas was actually a half-brother to Sir John, having been born in Sydney in 1808 to Sarah Please, the last Australian mistress of his and Sir John's father, Thomas, before he left for England in 1809. The younger Thomas helped Sir John run the estate at Regentville, but discreetly stayed in the background most of the time.

As the bands took a break around 11:30 p.m. guests were treated to a buffet dinner set out in adjacent rooms. An enormous range of offerings brought gasps of astonishment at the task of making choices from among the fifty different dishes. While Sir John's dining room was huge, it could not seat two hundred guests. Nonetheless there was no sacrifice in the number of culinary delights. Dishes for the first and second courses were spread out on tables on the front veranda with extra tables and chairs placed on the front lawn.

The first course consisted of a choice of two soups. The first was a vermicelli soup, prepared with tomatoes, onion, and garlic, while the second was a julienne soup, characterized by finely cut vegetables from Sir John's fields. Both soups were served in large silver tureens accompanied by fresh bread, baked on the premises.

The second course was somewhat heavier than the soup but still lighter than the actual entrée. Guests were served seafood; locally caught cod, trout, and lobster were available, either baked or broiled. Australian fishermen had discovered a plethora of fine sea foods in both salt and fresh water sources, and Sir John was proud to serve their catches. For discriminating palates Sydney oysters were a recommended treat.

The main entrée choices, because of their variety, were placed around the great table in the dining room, where waiters helped patrons fill their plates. Meat of many delicious forms tempted the clientele. Roasted lamb, beef, veal, and ham dishes took centre stage, with plates of rabbit, kangaroo, pheasant, quail, duck, and partridge scattered beyond. Each was clearly labeled in fine penmanship so no one had to show their ignorance of the cook's presentations. Silver serving spoons and forks exemplified Sir John's wealth and excellent taste. Thick gravy and Yorkshire pudding in ornate boats with ladles was plentifully available to accompany the roasts. Set between the main dishes were plates of vegetables including broccoli, cauliflower, potatoes, and carrots. Again, fresh bread in various forms was available at the end of the line.

Once their entrée was consumed, guests filed through the foyer where dessert was served. Consistent with options in previous courses, tantalizing choices made patrons inwardly groan with the sensual dilemma of making more decisions. Strawberries and cream, cherries, and other small stone fruits filled one table. Elsewhere, Neapolitan cakes consisting of layers of yellow, chocolate, and strawberry cake, with a glaze or simple buttercream frosting on top, competed with crepes, souffles, éclairs, and meringue treats. Sweet wine from Sir John's estate was available, as well as coffee, tea, hot punch, and water.

Conversation, when mouths weren't full, dwelled on the feast, with compliments flowing freely. Linen serviettes dabbed at ladies' lips ensuring no crumbs were missed and that their looks remained unsoiled. Sir John walked among the seated groups, both inside and outside, enjoying the constant adulation. He was delighted to bring several of the cooks out to join him at various stages and each was applauded for his skills.

Finally, guests had the opportunity to wash their sticky hands in bowls of lemon-scented water with fluffy towels for drying. Some patrons then retired to chairs and relaxed in the afterglow of fine food and drink. Inside, the bands took up again around 12:30 a.m. Those couples which felt replenished and revived took to the dance floor once more, although many of the men had gathered in the billiards room to puff on cigars. A number of women had formed a large group beyond the fountain where a young girl, a convict servant, was singing old homeland songs in a clear, strong voice. At times some of the watchers would join in to harmonize choruses, but the girl's voice was so beautiful the choruses usually faded out quickly. After every song there was a round of applause and several women were seen dabbing their eyes as nostalgic memories were recalled.

Sir John returned from the library, surveyed the dance floor, and moved outside to check on what was holding the ladies' attention. He stayed and applauded the young servant's rendition of "Home, Sweet Home," then headed back to the veranda.

"Ah, Misses Kingswood, Merriman, and Woolsley, such a lovely looking trio. Are you ladies enjoying yourselves? Not dancing at the moment? I trust you partook of dinner?"

Three heads nodded affirmation whereupon Sir John turned specifically to Judith and said, "Miss Merriman, I put your little present upstairs for safekeeping. Would you like to help me open it?"

"I'd be happy to, Sir John. I do hope you'll like it. Please lead the way."

And with that she nodded modestly to Ann and Sarah, and followed the Knight of Regentville up the central staircase.

With the dinner complete, the kitchen staff relaxed a little even though the chores of clearing dishes and washing them filled their time. The cooks smiled and exchanged appreciative comments that they had received and basked in the consequent realization of a positive outcome from their creativity and hard work. As reward they allowed the staff to each choose a leftover dessert and to have a glass of wine if they so desired. Of course some sampling had already taken place but it was nice to hear kind and caring words directly from the cooks.

With the dishes washed, wiped, and put away, many of the off-estate staff went outside the compound walls and meandered towards the river where they sat or lay down spread out along the banks with their drinks and cigarettes. The night was pleasantly warm and the moon three quarters full. Two couples wandered off into the orchards while small groups of four or more sat and shared tales of what they had observed in the behavior of guests, occasionally causing a prolonged laugh from descriptions of spilled drinks, stilted airs, stumbling dancers, jouncing bosoms, and groping male hand movements. Two of the convict men from the nearby Emu Plains camp dropped their clothes at the water's edge and plunged in, swimming across the river and back, no doubt wondering if this was a route to freedom and whether the time and opportunity were upon them. They emerged to the cheers of their fellow workers, coming to sit down amongst them again waiting for their bodies to dry before putting their clothes on once more. And as much as some of the girls were encouraged to also go skinny dipping, none felt sufficiently compelled to do so.

Meanwhile, in the shadows of the bigger trees deep in the orchard, far less modesty was being observed as primitive natural urges were satiated by highly charged pairs. For them, others didn't matter, and eventually it was only when the gentle morning sun touched their faces that they rose and wandered back to the sleepful mansion.

Much, much earlier, starting around 1:00 a.m., when guests decided to leave, their carriage drivers were awakened, the horses put in harness, given a drink of water and a couple of apples, and led back to the front door. Husbands and wives, many tipsy and burping, indecorously struggled into the carriages, trying to pompously uphold their dignity. The stable boy heartily slapped each horse's rump and was usually rewarded with a startled gasp or yell as the riders were thrown askew when the horse took off in a hurry. Another story to be shared with the other stable mates later.

Unless he was otherwise busy Sir John said goodbye to nearly everyone as they left. Summoned as the governor prepared to depart, he hurried down the stairs to thank the man for visiting and honouring his home and facilities. He waved goodbye at the front door then went back inside to the dance floor.

Judith found her friends waiting expectedly out by the fountain. Two voices spoke at the same time.

"Come on, my dear, we've been waiting well over an hour. What was he like? A gentleman through and through or a little bit on the wild side?"

"What did you talk about? How did he treat you? What is his bedroom like? So many questions, you must tell us, our curiosity runneth over, so to say."

"All I can tell you girls is that the rumours are true. There is no doubt that for fifty years old he is still exceptionally well endowed. And there is every good reason why he's called the king of cleavage and cunny. Oh boy! What an evening, what a man. I don't understand why Elizabeth Long didn't stay around. He has SO much to offer...!

"His room was gorgeous with the finest decorations in carpet, drapes, and bedspread, and simply the most beautifully ornate imported furniture. He treated me like a lady although frankly I don't remember much of what we talked about. He was very eager to try his key in my lock. Both of them, that is..."

"Judith, you are nothing but a whore and a tease! Lovable of course, but still a scalp collector. Well, maybe not scalps, but you know what I mean. I do and I don't want to know the details. What about you, Ann?"

"I don't believe I really want to know. Hearing intimate details may make me into a wicked woman, full of lust and longing. I think you should keep them to yourself, Judith."

"No matter what you would like to know, darlings, I fully intend to selfishly savour all the feelings and memories. They're mine, and mine alone. I will tell you only that the locket held all

the magic of the interlude. He was touched—no, overwhelmed—
by the picture inside. If he had wondered about me before, he no
longer did when he opened the case. He kissed my throat, then
my neck from side to side, then my bosom, and oh... well, I
promised I'd keep the details to myself, and so I shall.

"Well... on thinking about it, there was one amusing spot I
could share. He was very surprised to find my red hair was
matched in the downstairs region. I asked him what he had
expected—purple feathers? And he laughed so loudly I thought
people would be rushing in to see what was happening. Other
than that let's just say he's indefatigable both on the dance floor
and in the bedroom. I shall dream of him often I am sure...

"But tell me," she continued, "were either of you smart
enough to insist on a dance with young Thomas? He certainly is a
good-looking fellow and perhaps has some of the same traits as
his brother Sir John."

Two blank faces answered her question.

"Come on, darlings. How likely is such an opportunity to
come your way? Now follow me, for you are going to dance with
the young man. I shall make it happen. I don't know what you two
would do without me I'm sure..."

By 6:00 a.m. the last carriages were winding along the drive
towards the main gates, eastward bound, and servants and
helpers of all types had either gone home or were sleeping things
off on the river bank or elsewhere. Some were lying in the soft
grasses of close-by paddocks while three enterprising stable lads
were in the loft, not alone, exhausted from the merriment they
and their female companions had enjoyed in the recent hours.

A few select guests had been invited ahead of time to stay
over at the mansion and they peacefully slept the morning away.
Sir John, needing no more than four hours' rest, was in his study
by 8:00 a.m. having a cup of tea and checking his accounts before
most of the staff wandered in. They knew from experience that he
would be up before them, and envied him his ability to party all
night and be at business before most of them had their eyes open.
Today, a brunch would be served for the guests, given their

anticipated late rising. No doubt Sir John would be leading them on a detailed tour of the premises before sending them all home in the early afternoon, when normalcy would reign again.

For the staff it would soon be just another day coming down.

12. Theatre, Exploring, Census, Bushrangers

As predicted, one of the guests, probably Captain William John Dumaresq, at a later stage, anonymously offered yet another description of Sir John's manor in *The Australian*, March 1827, saying:

"On the right hand, and on a fine foreground stood the palace of Regentville, the noble seat of Sir John Jamison. This splendid building is beyond all comparisons. The finest thing of the kind in New South Wales, it stands on the top of a gentle hill, and presents a front to the long reach of the river and rich vale of Emu, of 180 feet, the centre building being 80 feet in length, and the two wings 50 feet each. Inside are comprised the library, baths. billiard-rooms. &c. &c., while the kitchens and servants offices are detached in the rear out of sight. Regentville is built of a fine free stone dug on the estate in the chastest style of Grecian architecture, and is no less remarkable in the interior for the good taste and richness of its decorations, and the profuse and constant hospitality of the noble owner."

Sir John's interests reflected a natural curiosity often displayed by great leaders. To some this was revealed in odd ways, sometimes reflecting the sublime, at other times the ridiculous.

The hospitable knight was happy to offer his home for an overnight stay to appropriate travellers on the Great Western road, especially those of substantial station who could be of value politically.

The drought of 1827 that had started the year before showed no letting up and the water level in the Nepean shrank accordingly. Still, as Bathurst grew, many farmers and merchants sought to move there, or at least visit, and the road across the mountains remained busy. Before the weather warmed towards the end of the year the Chief Justice, Francis Forbes, and his family came by Regentville on vacation. Sir John took the opportunity to introduce the Chief Justice to an incredibly unusual event.

Way across the river stood the penal camp of Emu Plains from which prisoners on chain gangs worked at hard labour to clear land and create roads along the fertile Nepean plains or construct relevant government buildings across the mountain slopes. Life was harsh in the camp with overseers known to be cruel and mean. However, a recent arrival at camp was an irrepressible little Cockney named James King, who had an amazing outgoing personality and charm, with talents from a past acting and comedic career. He succeeded in getting permission to establish a theatre at the camp and set himself up as architect, carpenter, manager, scene-painter, mechanic, and producer, as well as casting himself for the leading comic role in whatever plays were produced. He could neither read nor write, his method of learning his part being to listen to the play being read over and over.

He organized the building of a rough theatre, having the whole interior whitewashed with pipeclay. Rough benches served for seats. The camp superintendent supported the venture, supplying King with things he could not obtain on his own, for life in the camps was almost as tedious and boring for the officials in charge as it was for the convicts themselves. Through his scheme Jimmy became as popular with his oppressors as with the oppressed. He begged or stole remnants of bags and worn clothing, sewed them together, and painted his crude designs with pipeclay, charcoal, and coloured earths. Using tin cans he fashioned lamps and candlesticks, and cajoled the wicks, oil, and candles from the officials out of their rations from Government stores.

A number of convicts became enthused and rehearsed diligently for several different plays. Because practices and theatre construction had to be done in the evenings after days of heavy labour on the plains, and on Saturday, the members of the cast had very little rest or sleep. The existence of this theatrical venture among the convicts had been advertised throughout the area and most audiences consisted of the small settlers along the Nepean River, and their wives and children, people whose experience of theatrical production was limited to the exhibitions given by travelling mountebanks and strolling companies performing in barns.

Having been reassured of his own safety and that of his guests, Sir John decided to take the Chief Justice and both families to the final performance of the troupe. The list of pieces in which the convict-actors had been trained and rehearsed was given to the superintendent, who forwarded it to Sir John Jamison for selection. He chose "Raymond and Agnes," to be followed by "The Devil to Pay." Jimmy King worked hard to provide some extra flourishes including an orchestra of four instruments—a tin violin, a flute, a tambourine, and a great drum, from which, by some magic, a tolerable melody emerged.

The curtain went up, and the play went forward amid the enthusiastic plaudits of a friendly and uncritical audience. Everyone had fun, enjoying the heartfelt performances immensely, and gave the crew a standing ovation at the conclusion. While the delighted audience was preparing to leave, Sir John requested that the whole contingent of performers should be presented to him at the entrance. In a few minutes the actors, still in their fustian, were mustered in lines on each side of the crude staircase at the entrance to the building. Led by the superintendent, Sir John and his friends inspected the company, whence the ladies were especially intrigued to discover that 'Nell' was in reality a brawny bullock-driver with full whiskers. The man valued these so highly that he had resolutely refused to shave them for his part but had skillfully devised a special head-dress to hide them throughout the performance.

Sir John complimented one of the actors upon his performance and slipped a sovereign unobserved into his hand, telling him in a low tone that it was for himself. He then formally expressed his high satisfaction at the entertainment, and, giving the manager, Jimmy King, a present to share with the company, departed with his friends. This, with other gifts from members of the audience, enabled King to hand ten shillings to each of the musicians and fifteen shillings to each of the play-actors.

Once again Sir John had shown his support for the common man, in so doing no doubt creating a lesson for the Chief Justice at the same time. He clearly was of independent character.

Hobnobbing in high society, creating friendships with governors, using convicts for their skills, looking for solutions for societal problems in agriculture and elsewhere, and sharing his wealth, while continually adding to it through sales of cattle and sheep and other produce raised on his estate and grazing lands. Oblivious to standard social etiquette to a degree, but a believer in children, good food and wine, and having a good time. He entertained lavishly both at his Sydney town house and at his country estate, and in his affluence never lost an opportunity to extend hospitality to visitors to the colony, for whom he arranged outings, picnics, and other diversions. Indeed he lived like a genial and prosperous English squire, earning by his unlimited bounty the appropriate title, 'the hospitable Knight of Regentville.'

The big event of 1828 was the first full census in New South Wales, which at the time included the subsequently distinct states of Victoria and Queensland. It was taken in November and its purpose was to record all inhabitants of the colony, both convict and free. The forms used captured each individual's full name, age, place of residence, ship of arrival, religion, occupation, employer's name, and place of residence. Previous attempts to count the number of white people living on the Australian mainland were fatally compromised because military personnel were excluded from the musters, and free settlers could not be legally compelled to attend. Consequently, the population was greatly undercounted. Parliament passed an Act on 29 July 1827 compelling all inhabitants of the colony, convict or free, to be recorded.

Indigenous people were not included in the census but the white population totaled 36,508, of which 20,780 were free and 15,728 were convicts. Only six hundred thirty were in the Queensland area. Twenty-four percent of the population was born in the colony, and seventy-five percent were male, while sixty-nine percent described themselves as Protestant and thirty percent were listed as Catholic. Associated with Sir John's name were one hundred eight individuals living in the districts of Airds, Evan (containing Regentville), and Bathurst, and the towns of Luskintyre and Anambah. Over one hundred of these were convicts, a few free by servitude, some with tickets of leave. Men from other properties were recorded simply because they happened to be visiting on the Census day. Conversely, not all Regentville workers were listed as some were absent elsewhere. John Griffiths was named but not his daughter Mary.

Not only were details on individuals collected but also information on stock holdings, and the location of all the gangs and road parties and men at government establishments. One of the most comprehensive censuses undertaken in early years of the colony, it gave authorities valuable information for various planning purposes. Sir John managed 19,350 acres at Regentville, of which some 9,840 had been cleared and two hundred sixty-five cultivated. He ran one hundred sixty-eight horses, eighteen hundred horned cattle, and thirty-four hundred sheep.

In spite of his differences with the government Jamison always exhibited great public spirit and was prominent in most movements aimed at the improvement of prevailing conditions or at the redressing of an evil. Throughout his colonial life he devoted his time, wealth, and influence to the introduction of the free institutions of England into the colony. No one would characterize him as a statesman per se, despite the activities described. In some ways he was an enigma, with different assessments based on each viewer's personal interaction or engagement. He could be highly outspoken on select positions and perceptions that were often inappropriate or even erroneous, yet amazingly humble and supportive on others. His magnanimity showed in a multitude of different ways, whether it was to build a bridge across the Nepean or to support explorers.

Also in late 1828 an increasing number of tales from aborigines visiting Sydney suggested that there existed an extensive sea in the interior of the country. This possibility excited the population because it had long been supposed, from the absence of any river of great magnitude emanating from such a large continent, that there must be some extensive morass or reservoir of water somewhere inland. Should such a source be found navigable it would be of massive importance in helping open up the interior and preventing more settlers from moving to Van Diemen's Land instead.

Sir John offered to finance an expedition to check out the possibility of this inland lake or sea. Further information from aborigines in Bathurst suggested it was a salt-water lake some three hundred miles away from that town, based on which it was conjectured that it could be an inlet of the sea from the direction of Spencer's Gulf. Sir John sent his brother Thomas to arrange interviews of one of the natives who purported to know about the lake. Three separate trusted local Bathurst aborigines talked to the visitor and described a long and hazardous journey to reach the lake. Supposedly along the way explorers would pass through an area called Cowel Swamp which, because of the drought, was now dry but was usually full of water. The inland lake was called Walambingie, and was now referenced as a fresh, rather than salt, water lake in which all sorts of animals and fish lived. It fed a stream flowing to the south.

Thomas returned to Regentville and discussed his findings with Sir John. Experience of past dealings with natives and the contradictory form of their input led Sir John to distrust what he was hearing. Together with his brother he assessed in greater detail the potential costs and benefits from a successful outcome. His doubts weighed heavily, however, and with much regret in the end he felt compelled to abandon the provocative idea of the expedition.

It's not clear which lake the natives were talking about. Lake Garnpung could have been an option, but if distances and timing were highly underestimated, another possibility could have been Lake Alexandrina, the discovery of which came a little later by Sturt and McLeay, who travelled down the Murrumbidgee and Murray rivers. Attempting to reach that lake by the route the natives had suggested would have meant certain death for explorers at the time and Sir John's decision not to proceed was appropriate. No one blamed him for his unwillingness to fund an expedition when the information was broadly published in the newspapers of January 1829.

In the heat of that month, on Saturday the 10th, Mary bore Sir John their first son. They named him Robert Thomas. Children born in summer were at high risk in the early days of the colony. The massive heat didn't help as infants became weak and just couldn't cope. Diarrhea, dehydration, and debility were increasingly common reasons ascribed to young deaths. Pneumonia and whooping cough were usually diseases of colder weather, but even they affected some in summer. Scarlatina and diphtheria could strike at any time, and while inoculation offerings were just starting to become available, the general public was not convinced of their efficacy. Medicine by many standards was still fairly primitive. In any event young Robert survived due to constant attention, many cool towels on his body, lots of hand-fanning, and the medical capabilities of his father.

Around this time Sir John decided to get more serious about growing grapes for wine. He already had a small vineyard but hired a German emigrant named Meyer to lay out a terraced vineyard at Regentville using the latest practices from Germany and France. Unfortunately, Meyer was not the expert he claimed to be. He was allotted a hillside facing due south, with soil that was a mixture of sand and yellow clay. The large number of small terraces he deployed were mistakenly constructed too narrow for the roots, which became blocked by the stone retaining walls. The grapevine cuttings were placed in the terraces without any rich soil or manure. The resultant vineyard was beautifully picturesque as it was enclosed by hedges of china rose and lemon. It contained between thirty and forty thousand vines of more than two hundred different grape varieties. An image of the vineyard was subsequently recorded in a pencil drawing by Conrad Martens, but the wine produced years later was not of good quality.

Governor Darling was running into more and more opposition ever since his unlawful change in 1827 of two convicts' sentences to a form of torture that led to the death of one of them. Two newspapers, *The Australian*, published by William Charles Wentworth and Robert Wardell, and *The Monitor*, published by Edward Smith Hall, kept up relentless attacks on the governor's capabilities. Under public pressure he was forced to ultimately release the second prisoner. Darling's subsequent attempts to muffle the newspapers failed badly initially, but later, Hall was gaoled and A. E. Hayes, editor of *The Australian*, was fined. Darling was then rebuked by the under-secretary of state, Viscount Howick, in England for attempting to repress free discussion, and as a result he was relieved of duty in 1831. His departure for England was greeted by public rejoicing.

Certain merchants, officials, and other influential patrons, including Sir John, stood behind the governor. When a demand by various writers for his impeachment was forwarded to the Home Government authorities in June 1829, the supporters felt compelled to speak out publicly. Sir John was the author of a letter that was signed by fifty-eight individuals:

> To His Excellency Lieutenant General
> RALPH DARLING, Governor in Chief,
> &c. &c. &c.
> May it please your Excellency,

> We, the undersigned, Landed Proprietors and Merchants, resident in the Colony, beg leave to approach your EXCELLENCY, with unfeigned expressions of duty and regard, and to state, that although we have hitherto remained silent, yet it has been with deep regret that we have long observed every measure of your EXCELLENCY grossly vituperated by licentious public writers, in a manner calculated to inflame the minds of the lower orders of the community against your EXCELLENCY'S administration, and to produce discontent and insubordination among the prisoners of the Crown, for no other purpose than to promote the interested views of such writers. As, however, we now find that charges against Your EXCELLENCY have been forwarded to the Home Government, in the form of an Impeachment, we can no longer refrain from an expression of our sentiments.

> .

> It is but justice to state, that we have long observed Your EXCELLENCY patiently sacrificing your health and comfort, by an indefatigable attention to the difficult and arduous duties of the important charge committed to your care by our gracious Sovereign. And it is gratifying to us to acknowledge, amongst the important

results of Your EXCELLENCY'S labours, many improved arrangements in the various public Departments of the Colony.

We are convinced that every act of Your EXCELLENCY'S administration has emanated from the purest motives, and in the particular case upon which the Impeachment is founded, we feel confident that the measures adopted were not only judicious, but at that time imperative, and the result has been the most satisfactory.

We deny that the political opinions promulgated by the opposition journals are those of the more intelligent classes of the community, or that these publications form any criterion by which the justness of Your EXCELLENCY'S measures can be appreciated.

Having thus conveyed to Your EXCELLENCY our feelings, we beg to express our sincere wish that Your EXCELLENCY'S measures may be justly appreciated by the Home Government, and that you may long continue in the administration of the high office you now fill.

Darling was not impeached, and for his support Sir John was returned to the magistracy before the governor returned home.

Sir John's life was incredibly busy. He owned two households, managed thousands of acres of land and thousands of livestock, had well over one hundred convicts in his employ, and catered to one or more mistresses and several children at any point in time. He constantly bought new acreage, applied for extra convict labour, sold lamb, mutton, and beef, plus wool, wheat, and vegetables, and raced horses. He was on the board of the Bank of New South Wales and other various important associations and managed frequent ongoing correspondence with officials both in Sydney and London. And of course every once in a while he threw a dinner, or a party, for his friends, and never hesitated to entertain significant visitors trekking across the Blue Mountains. Every now and then he had a criminal issue to attend to. Someone would steal something off the estate, or a convict labourer would go missing and he'd have to ask the authorities to investigate.

When Sir John built at Regentville six years previously, he had advertised for twenty tenant farmers to occupy plots in the southwestern corner of his estate. This emulated British practices and worked to both tenant and landlord's favour. But nothing could have prepared one pair of tenants or their landlord for an unusual event that occurred in September.

About midnight one Friday evening two men knocked on the door and pushed themselves into the home of Barney Hoe and John Dunn, who lived about a mile away from the mansion. The strangers stated they were constables from Windsor and Penrith and demanded to know if any bushrangers were hiding inside. After receiving assurance that no bushrangers were there, one of the strangers locked the door on the inside, and told the old men that they had now two very desperate bushrangers in their dwelling. They were ordered to remain quiet, otherwise their brains would he blown out with a blunderbuss and a double-barreled pistol, pointed at them and a young boy, now sitting up in bed.

One of the robbers was dressed in a blue jacket, dark waistcoat and trousers, worn-out half boots, white shirt, coloured neckerchief, and black hat. He was short at about four feet nine inches tall, with brown hair, well featured, but with a dark complexion and a melancholy countenance, athletic and active, and about thirty years of age. He was armed with a blunderbuss and four pairs of pistols, secured in a belt under his jacket. The man other was low-set, younger, about five feet six inches tall, broad-faced, with a scar on his lip and under the left nostril, flaxen hair, of fair complexion and brown, rather freckled. He wore a blue jacket, light cord trousers, a coloured waistcoat, half boots, white shirt, no neckerchief, and a black hat, and was armed with a double-barreled pistol, and three pairs of pistols fastened to a belt round his body, under his jacket.

The taller man seated himself on a stool, with his back against the door, and pointed the blunderbuss and double-barreled pistol at the owners of the hut, whilst the other robber collected all the food available, consisting of four hams, some bacon and salted pork, thirty-five pounds of flour, one pound of tea, sixteen pounds of sugar, and seventy pounds of tobacco. They added a blanket and two pairs of trousers. The robbers then decanted a bottle of rum they brought with them into a tin, and tied the owners' hands behind their backs, fastened their knees and ankles, and then bound them back to back. Amazingly, the robbers then baked a cake, and fried enough pork for their supper. Afterwards the shorter man piled wood on the fire until the blaze nearly reached the roof thatch. When Old Hoe pleaded to not be burned alive the taller bushranger threw a bucket of water on the flames, saving the house and occupants.

This chap, who appeared to be an Englishman, found fault with his partner, who spoke broad Irish, and swore, with murderous threats in all his actions. Before leaving, the Englishman returned Hoe the trousers, and left a portion of pork, flour, tea, and sugar for breakfast, then disappeared with their booty. The fact that the hut owners were able to give such precise descriptions of their assailants led police to conclude that the men were the notorious bushrangers Jack Donahue and 'Darky' Underwood, wanted for a spate of crimes in Sydney and the countryside.

Jack Donahue was born in Dublin, Ireland, in 1804. He was often in trouble with the police for his political activities to gain independence, and in 1824 was sent to Sydney on the convict ship *Ann and Amelia*, which arrived on 2 January, 1825. He worked for two different farmers but in between served time on a chain gang. With two other men, George Kilroy and Bill Smith, he held up some carts on the Richmond Road. The police soon caught them and the court sentenced them to death. As he was being taken back to gaol in Sydney, Jack escaped. The government offered a reward of twenty pounds for his capture.

In August 1828, Donahue and a gang of eight robbed houses south of Bathurst. A police group nearly captured him near Goulburn. They shot at the gang, killing several gang members, but once again Donahue escaped and was not seen for several months. He next appeared in the Nepean River valley around the towns of Liverpool, Penrith, Windsor, Parramatta, and Liberty Plains. Donahue, 'Darky' Underwood, and an escaped convict named Jack Walmsley robbed the Reverend Samuel Marsden near Windsor. The government increased the reward to £50 and in

April 1830, Governor Darling made a special law to try to stop
bushranging. Under it the police could arrest anyone, and enter
and search houses without a warrant.

Almost exactly one year after the Regentville attack, a group
of police and soldiers searching for Donahue found him camped by
a creek at Bringelly, a small town well south of Regentville.
Donahue was shot in the neck and forehead and died. The other
two got away but it wasn't long before Walmsley was found and
killed. Two years later in 1832 Darky Underwood was also finally
tracked down and shot and killed.

Sir John's interests varied widely, another being in the
advancement of education. On Australia Day, 26 January 1830, he
and a number of dignitaries were present at the laying of the
foundation stone for Sydney College, later known as the Sydney
Free Grammar School. Guns at the battery fired a salute to
commemorate the landing of the First Fleet forty-two years earlier
and a procession from the Royal Hotel marched up George and
Market streets to Hyde Park. The president of the college was the
Chief Justice Francis Forbes, supported on his right by Sir John, and
on the left by the Reverend Dr. Dunmore Lang. The master of
ceremonies, the secretary, and the treasurer came behind,
followed by the nine committee members and the nine trustees.

The foundation stone was lowered into a prepared
excavation, and with a silver trowel presented to him by the
trustees, the president deposited several coins beneath the stone
and then performed the official ceremony. The inscription on the
stone reads:

> "This foundation stone of Sydney College-, an institution
> founded for the vigorous and pious promotion of polite literature and
> the liberal arts, among the youth of Australia, was laid by Francis
> Forbes, Chief Justice of New South Wales, on an auspicious day,
> viz. the 26th of January, in the year of our Lord 1830: in the happy
> reign of George IV, Lieutenant General Ralph Darling being
> Governor of New South Wales."

The obese and unlamented king, who was recognized only for rebuilding Buckingham Palace and Windsor Castle, was to die of a heart attack six months later at just under sixty-eight years old. He was succeeded by his younger brother William IV, since his one legitimate daughter, Princess Charlotte of Wales, died giving stillbirth in 1817.

By Christmas 1830, Mary knew another child was on the way. Celebrations that year were more festive than ever. Sir John was growing in stature in the political and economic arena, while at the same time becoming enormously richer. The severe drought had broken and his grazing pastures were filled with increased births of calves, lambs, and piglets destined to grow fat and to feed the expanding population of the colony as more and more free settlers emigrated to the new land.

Life was good.

13. Benevolence and Arrogance

Life continued to be good as 1831 rolled on, especially with the birth of Sir John's second son, William Henry, 8 June. Harriet, from Sir John's first Sydney liaison, and now twelve years old, came to live at the estate and the Jamison/Cain/Griffiths family settled into a routine.

John's responsibilities as president of the Agricultural and Horticultural Society included providing a report summarizing the previous year's findings and accomplishments. Unseasonable lack of rain in July and August affected wheat crops, which recovered but then were dashed with heavy frosts in early November. On the other hand hops had done well, tobacco plantings had increased but production of flax and hemp declined. More grapevines had been planted. On the livestock side cattle numbers were growing out of sight with prices for beef falling accordingly. Mutton prices had fallen but wool prices had held up as European wool growers faced increasing costs not found in Australia with extensive and rich grazing lands.

Agricultural practices and processes were changing with antipodean experience, and in looking forward Sir John noted that he hoped "the period is not far distant, when we shall manufacture all the woollen goods we require, distil our spirituous liquors, brew as much beer as we want, and above all, make the whole of the wine and oil we stand in need of." He lauded the discovery conquests of Sturt and McLeay, and in an impassioned conclusion of his report to the governor and fellow officers he suggested that future discoveries of rivers emptying to the coast would "open the most extensive tract of country, in one of the finest climates the world can boast of, for the reception of millions of emigrants." His particular vision was focused on rivers to the west which never materialized as he had hoped, but the millions of emigrants came anyway.

Sir John was not only a visionary but a practical man of the land as well. He truly desired to help farmers become more efficient and productive in their holdings, and to that end continually passed on impactful local experiences as well as those from overseas. In his previous annual report for the year 1829, he had presented information designed to help every farmer in the land by describing an experiment he'd conducted on clearing stumps from desired areas.

The aborigines knew the country as a land of forests. To the white man many of these forests stood on rich soil that could be used for income and profit through agriculture. So the forests were cleared with axes and cross-cut saws, and the resultant timbers used to build homes. More clearing occurred as roads were built from the farms to the villages that sprang up around the agricultural centres. But the clearing process left ugly stumps, except where trees were totally uprooted due to storms. Removing the stumps was a job for convicts in government camps. With only hoes, spades, and axes at their disposal it was definitely hard labour.

Sir John indicated that in 1825 six hundred acres of forest timber were felled on his property but remained untouched until September 1828. Thirty labourers were then employed to grub-up the stumps and burn off the timber. The effort took so long, however, that it was abandoned well before completion. As an experiment, twenty acres were identified for burning but with an extra arrangement whereby a considerable number of logs were rolled close around each stump beforehand. The trees felled had been a mixture of iron bark, box, stringy bark, gum, and apple. The whole twenty acres were set on fire one evening and the following morning it was found that about one-third of the whole stumps had burned out even to the extreme points of the roots many feet underground. Many localized stumps were still burning, and in five days ninety-nine percent of the stumps were completely burnt. The method was then applied to four hundred acres with similar success. He noted that gum and stringy bark trees often needed fires to be relit.

As a consequence of this portion of the report Sir John was awarded a gold medal by the London Society for the Encouragement of Arts and Manufactures. His practice of extirpating stumps became the default efficient method of clearing stumps from then on.

Of course being such a public figure, everyone took notice of Sir John's remarks. Two years after his report, upon publication of the clearing process in the *Sydney Gazette*, a Tasmanian, Mr. U Fidkin, had a letter published in the *Colonial Times* that presented strong evidence that he had invented the fire-in-the-stump method of clearing twelve years earlier in 1817 on his own land in Liverpool, New South Wales. The account of his method also claimed the process was used to clear the streets of Liverpool itself. Whether Sir John heard about this years later before trying it himself will never be known. In any event he got the credit for bringing it to public light.

Sir John wasn't universally liked. There were times when he seemed to abuse the powers he held. After he was restored to the magistracy there was an incident in November that didn't sit well with certain country folk. Magistrates were officials whose function was to execute the law in the sense of authorizing or denying applications for various civil activities brought to them by local residents. The owner of a small Inn in Emu Plains, Mr. Wilson, was denied a liquor licence due to the small size of his inn. His landlord built a new, larger inn and fenced in some property to stop cattle trespassing on his land. Sir John told the innkeeper that his application would be denied again unless the landlord took down the fence he had erected since it blocked a path his cattle used to avoid a higher ground passage. Debate in court was heated as other magistrates felt Sir John was going beyond the law in dismissing the application since the innkeeper did not own the land where the fence was placed. The landlord realized he was in the right legally and not required to take the fence down, but seeing that the other magistrates were unwilling to challenge Sir John, indicated if the fence was in Sir John's way he could knock it down. So acknowledged, Sir John immediately granted the innkeeper his licence.

There is a saying that "Not all is fair in war or business." Sir John exemplified it once again. While clearly looking after his personal interests, at the same time, and on the other hand, he was actively promoting trial by jury and a representative parliamentary assembly by leading petitions to the king and governor. Long debates and discussion took place in meetings in Sydney and Parramatta with long and tiresome editorials in newspapers clarifying, edifying, and challenging the proposals. Sir John in this respect was the champion and chief representative of the immigrant settler class, agitating for reform to benefit the common man. A man of great contrasts. On one hand, highly intelligent, and statesmanlike in his untiring efforts to enhance the country he lived in, not just for fellow farmers, but for everyone. Perhaps he foresaw, better and clearer than anyone else, the end of the convict regime and the emergence of a new society, for while he hobnobbed with the aristocracy peddling his thoughts and influence, he also worked with the convicts and danced with the natives.

And yet in contrast he could flaunt common practices and decency for personal gain. Whether it was by continually living as a playboy hedonist leading to conceiving children out of wedlock, or by putting his own interests first over official doctrines, there was an arrogance about the man that some found regrettable, if not unforgivable. He created attention in many different ways.

At the corner of Churchill and George streets in Sydney, an unusually shaped large triangular piece of public land not built upon, marked the corner and was a help to cart drivers who had to negotiate the sharp turn into George Street at the bottom of the very steep and dangerous aspect of Churchill. Governor Brisbane, in office from 1821 to 1825, had granted the building beyond the triangular patch to Sir John, who in late 1831 claimed he was selling the patch and the buildings to a Mr. Lyons, who intended to build on the triangular patch. Citizens were annoyed at this presumption of property ownership and complained in the press about how "a man of great wealth who lent money to officers" could violate the understandings and approved public rights that had been in place since the colony was founded. Though the complaints were aired, the building went up.

Out at Regentville the population kept growing as Sir John increased his acreage, ran more sheep and cattle, expanded the orchard and grain fields, and purchased and trained new horses. Extra convicts were assigned to him and their camp started to become crowded. At the same time more bedrooms at the mansion were starting to be used on a permanent basis as five of his children now resided there.

It was as if overnight Regentville had become a little metropolis. Certainly it was the social centre of the surrounding rural area, for Sir John never stopped entertaining and became increasingly famous for his generous hospitality.

14. Butcher-man

George Dent had been born in the rural village of Erith in Kent, east of London and south of the Thames. His mother died when he was four and his father, William, then worked at two jobs to support George and his two elder sisters, Mariann and Sarah. Sarah was developmentally challenged but George, two years younger, was her ever-present nurturer. Mariann, born two years before Sarah, grew into an accomplished pickpocket, augmenting the family income with a few coins every now and then. At fifteen she found a position as a maid at a young family's house in London. George, starting at age ten, worked hard over long hours, carrying bags of coal from the warehouses on the wharves to select customers' coal cellars in the village. In so doing he developed the broad shoulders and strength of his father. Bullies who tried to take advantage of Sarah often ran afoul of George's fighting abilities, for he was afraid of no one, no matter if they be older or bigger.

At age fifteen he became a butcher's apprentice and over the next six years grew in experience to serve as a fully accomplished butcher's assistant. His strength allowed him to carry select carcasses directly from the market to the shop, avoiding the costs of cartage for his proprietor with whom he also lodged. To supplement his earnings and to offset some of the taunts thrown at him as someone without skills in accounting or engineering, he also became a back-streets pugilist. He was good, with strength augmented by speed, a decisive punching capability, and a physique which could take heavy blows. On finally defeating the local champion he was offered the chance to join a stable of boxers run by a vivacious widower with an appetite for sexual trysts with virulent men.

His father pleaded with him to stop fighting, as he saw signs of unwelcome behavior in his son who now ran around with a new crowd submitting to different morals and interests than those with which his father had raised him. George had long forgone looking after Sarah, although he gave money to his father whenever he could. On being told that Sarah was dying he raced home, feeling terrible that he had forsaken the sister who had lived and depended on him so much in her early life. His heart broke when he saw how his beautiful sister had become just skin and bones, but there was nothing to be done as she slowly wasted away, except to absorb more and more guilt and fight harder for bigger prizes as his only outlet of escape from same.

Mariann married a banker and soon became pregnant. She was the upright citizen and the apple of her father's eye. Contrarily, one of George's more depraved comrades talked him in to stealing all the belongings of his proprietor and landlord. What seemed like a simple and straightforward plan went awry when the landlord's son came home early from school and fetched a constable. George was sent to Middlesex gaol, and while waiting for his trial his sister died, adding to his misery. With some of his fight winnings given to his father, he helped buy a memorial headstone for her grave at St. John the Baptist Church of England in their home town. Mariann and her husband were present as Sarah was laid to rest beside her mother and James, buried so long ago. George's eyes were constantly blurred and he only slept out of exhaustion.

At his trial 12 May, 1831, George was readily convicted and sentenced to be hung. But as it came to pass, he was granted a reprieve 'at King William IV's pleasure' and sentenced to life 'transportation' to Australia. He spent another month in the Middlesex gaol before being transferred to one of the hulks in the Thames in anticipation of eventual transportation to the Antipodes. The *Retribution* became his new abode, and he joined the prisoner gangs working at hard labour seven hours a day on the foreshores of the Thames. Some days they dug canals or built walls around the Woolwich Arsenal, other days they drove in posts to protect the riverbanks from erosion, and on others they added infrastructure in the form of wharves, pathways, and roads along the banks. George's conditioning helped him tolerate the harsh conditions far better than most of the men.

Many prisoners had spent over eighteen months in a hulk. The authorities were always keen to keep down the costs of these floating prisons. They wanted to avoid giving prisoners a better quality of life than the poor had outside the hulks, and accordingly the quality of the prisoners' food was therefore kept as low as possible. The monotonous daily meals consisted chiefly of ox-cheek, either boiled or made into soup, peas, and bread or biscuit. The biscuits were often mouldy and green on both sides. Two days a week, the meat was replaced with oatmeal and cheese. Each prisoner had two pints of beer four days a week, and poorly filtered water, drawn from the river, on the others. Sometimes, the captain of a hulk would allow the convicts to plant vegetables in plots near the Arsenal. This attempt to add something extra to the poor diet of the prisoners depended on the goodwill of the individual in charge. In George's case, no such extra privileges were experienced.

At Christmas, father and Mariann came to visit, bringing fresh ham and some delicious plum pudding to share. "You look well, Father," said George. "I am sorry to have let you down and brought shame upon the family. I have no idea what really lies ahead for me once I get to Australia, but I promise you that I will not fight for a living again if I ever gain my freedom. You know I can never return to England and I don't expect you to make the long trip to come see me. The only thing I would ask is that if I do somehow make good down there that you might send me some of my money to help me get my feet well established. Otherwise it is totally yours.

"And Mariann, your pregnancy sits well. You simply glow and remind me of your younger sister, bless her soul. There is a radiance shining about you. I am so very happy for you and hope things proceed well over the next five months. But I must ask one small favour. If you deliver a boy please name him anything but George. I couldn't bear to think that some innocent lad would bear my name."

Father spoke up: "Son, I'm glad to see you still look healthy despite the prison conditions. And I thank you for your vow. I know you will keep it. You are only twenty-two and there is a lot of life to live yet. Always protect yourself but don't instigate trouble. Let others be the troublemakers no matter how strongly you feel about things."

With a final hug, Father added, "I wish you good luck and I'll be happy to forward funds should you get a pardon and become a free man. That I would like to hear."

"And I have a strange thought to share with you, brother," said Mariann, "for I know in my heart there is a good man deep inside you and I believe you will bring him to the fore and he will guide you in Australia. Perhaps you are actually being given a new opportunity although it may not seem so this minute. I just have this feeling in my soul that life in Australia may end up even better than it would be if you stayed here in London. I'll pray that it is so. Do not forget to write to me and your father."

A month later, George was unexpectedly called forward from the musty, stale confines of the *Retribution* and taken in chains by cart to The Downs in Kent, where he was placed on board the *John I*, a typical barque of four hundred and sixty four tons converted for convict transportation. Originally slated to leave on 26 January 1832, bad weather and extra repairs held the ship back. Finally, on Tuesday 7 February 1832, under the command of Captain Sam Lowe and Surgeon Mr. James Lawrence, the *John I* eased from her moorings and headed into the Channel to commence the long voyage to Sydney. No one stood on the wharf and waved goodbye, no tears were shed by wailing relatives. Other than a few dogs barking, the only other noise filling the gloomy silence of the prisoners' quarters was the swish of water breaking from the boat's bows and the mournful creaking of the timbers as she picked up speed.

Like most convict ships of the times the *John I* suffered through massive storms, great calms, and oppressive heat as she made her way southwest towards South America then southeast towards South Africa. Conditions for convicts were no different from those on other boats, more suited to animals than humans, but they met the transport rules of the British penal system. Captain Sam Lowe and Surgeon Mr. James Lawrence managed a peaceful journey until a couple of rebellious convicts decided to set fire to the prison where they were housed. The two men, Samuel Dodds and Michael Buosey, secretly smuggled a live coal into the prison and with it ignited a small pile of oakum and chips close to the foremast. The alarm was given when smoke penetrated into the hospital and rose through the fore hatchway. The fire was promptly extinguished, having done no damage beyond charring the prison floor.

Dodds and Buosey were punished with whippings and there the incident might have ended had not another convict, John Clifton, been heard to remark that he wished "the ship was on fire from stem to stern." Rightly or wrongly, Surgeon Lawrence believed that Clifton had been involved in the kindling of the fire and, as punishment for his remark, ordered him next morning to walk the deck with a bed on his back for two hours. This curious punishment took place under the supervision of two convicts selected for the purpose by Mr. Lawrence. Clifton was supposedly leg-ironed, although the two supervisors said later that he had on only one leg iron. When the punishment started at 10:00 a.m. Clifton's bed had not been brought up from below and Mr. Lawrence ordered him to walk at a quick pace. Whether the two supervising convicts misinterpreted the surgeon's order is not clear but when Mr. Lawrence observed Clifton about three quarters of an hour later, the unfortunate man, though still bed-less, was running, not walking, around the deck.

It was a rare, somewhat warm, day with the thermometer in the shade of the cuddy registering seventy degrees Fahrenheit, so the surgeon immediately told Clifton, in the hearing of the supervising convicts, that he was to walk and not run. The story reaching all the other prisoners' ears became confused at this point. Clifton's bed was finally brought on deck and he lugged it around on his back only during the final fifteen minutes of his punishment. When his ordeal finished at noon Clifton was perspiring freely and was highly fatigued. He sat on the deck and drank water and wine supplied by his two supervisors. Later in the afternoon the surgeon found him alone by the mast, cold and shivering. The man was at once carried below but he died at about 4:00 p.m. The surgeon felt that the wine he drank while he was in a distressed condition from the exertion of his punishment was what had caused his death.

Many of the prisoners were already weak from the trying and humiliating conditions back in prison cells and hulks before even embarking on their transportation ship. On board, rations were small and not well balanced in their offerings, with salted pork the mainstay. If and when fresh fish were caught along the way they went first to the captain and his crew, then cabin passengers, if any, and finally as a last resort to convicts. Underneath the main deck the pitch and roll of the ship was exaggerated and some men never really fully contained their seasickness. Sanitation was primitive and illness and death were not uncommon amongst the men.

The lack of appropriate care for Clifton by the surgeon was a point of anger for most prisoners, who had little faith in Mr. Lawrence's commitment to their welfare. Once around the Cape, it was almost a direct easterly course, albeit slightly southerly, past the islands of St. Paul and Amsterdam and on to the great Australian southern coastline. In the cold temperatures of the southern Indian Ocean two more fierce storms occurred almost on top of one another. Coughs and colds were everywhere present as the drafty conditions increased exposure to the harsh elements. One elderly weak man died despite the surgeon's multiple attempts to keep him alive, and the mood of the remaining convicts became sour and ugly again. It stayed that way until the captain announced that they had passed Cape Leeuwin and were now in the shadow of Australia.

Three weeks later in the middle of the morning the ship rounded the Sydney heads, fired off its arrival cannon, and waited for the pilot ship to pull alongside. It was Friday 8 June 1832.

The next morning the prisoners were told to fetch their belongings and in small groups were taken to the lone jetty by tender. Most welcomed the weak sunshine, although walking on terra firma was as difficult as they had been told it would be, and many found it easier to sit on the ground while they waited for their fellow travelers to be rowed ashore.

They were lined up without chains and marched half a mile under heavy guard to the Hyde Park Barracks, which formed the general depot at the time for receiving all prisoners, and where next steps were determined. Two days after arrival George was summoned from his cell to the office of the warden.

"George Dent, you are now a convict serving at His Majesty's pleasure in the penal colony of New South Wales. Because of the nature of the crime you committed you may never return to England, but you may be eligible in fourteen years for a Certificate of Pardon should your behavior be exemplary. Most men who arrive here will be assigned to chain gangs in Sydney or elsewhere. They'll be helping to build the necessary infrastructure for development of towns and villages. However, you will be more fortunate. Your profession is butcher. Correct?"

"Yes sir."

"How long since you were active as such?"

"Fourteen months, sir."

"Is that how you came by your deformed thumb?"

"Yes sir. Early in my apprenticeship I was a little off target with the chopping blade. The thumb was flattened and cut severely and my nail had to be removed. I was lucky the thumb didn't need amputation." George said nothing more, waiting for the warden to continue.

"The commander of the garrison on board the *John I* has spoken well of you, and given that you have a profession, unlike the majority of your fellow convicts, the colony can make good use of your skills.

"There is an open assignment for which I shall enter your name. Forty miles west of Sydney near the town of Mulgoa by Penrith way, Sir John Jamison has established an estate named Regentville. It so happens that among the latest set of requests he has submitted, there is one for a butcher on his property. You seem to match his needs. You probably would prefer to stay in Sydney, but there are no butcher positions available at the moment. This happens to be one of two in country areas.

"You either accept this job or join a chain gang. There are no other options for you, young man. Which will it be?"

"I'll travel west sir and take my chances. I was raised in Kent with its wide open fields of grain and vegetables, although I've spent the last seven years in London city. I think I could enjoy being in the countryside again."

"I don't think it will be a picnic, Mr. Dent, and your work and attitude will be monitored. Be aware. My advice for you is simple. Do what you are asked and more, do not complain, and do not cause trouble.

"We do not like to keep convicts in the barracks any longer than necessary. Tomorrow at noon you will be marched to the docks to catch the boat to Parramatta. After that it will be a buggy ride to Regentville. You will of course be accompanied by one of the soldiers and will be his prisoner until you are delivered to Sir Jamison."

Standing up in a sign of dismissal, the warden extended his hand in a generous gesture. "Good luck, Mr. Dent. I hope you find your place in this fine land."

Between 1788 and 1792, almost five thousand convicts reached Sydney on the First, Second, and Third Fleets. During the long wars with Revolutionary and Napoleonic France, British authorities were fully occupied in seeing that the nation survived, and ships were obviously needed for purposes other than convict transportation. The transportation practice faltered somewhat and only about seven thousand convicts, or four hundred per year, reached eastern Australia from 1793 to 1810.

However, the Allies' victory over Napoleon at Waterloo in 1815 brought an end to the drawn-out northern hemisphere fighting. This led to tens of thousands of soldiers and sailors returning to a Britain suffering economic decline and also facing the full effects of the Enclosure movement, whereby small land holdings were amalgamated into larger, privately owned ones, plus the effects of the Industrial Revolution, which further dispossessed the rural labouring classes. With the population increasing, unemployment high, and poverty widespread, crime accelerated and the courts sentenced offenders to transportation in ever increasing numbers. From 1816 to 1825 an average of twenty-six hundred convicts a year reached eastern Australia. For the next ten years, this climbed to around five thousand per year. Between 1821 and 1830, thirty-two thousand five hundred came; and from 1831 to 1840 another fifty-one thousand including the two hundred on *John I.*

By 1832 when George arrived, extensive exploration across the southeast corner of the country had already been undertaken. Sydney had become a very large town in its own right with a resident population (excluding convicts) of approximately fifteen thousand, in fact far bigger and more prosperous than many English towns, with outlying areas like Goulburn, Newcastle, Campbelltown, and Parramatta also growing at significant rates.

No longer was Sydney just a penal colony, but rather a growing city that happened to have a penal colony in its midst. Some married convicts were even assigned to their free spouses if they were there. Originally, the populace back home in England was deliberately not informed of this particular arrangement, in order to maintain continued justification of the penalty of transportation for the vile and depraved criminals in their midst. In eastern Australia, transportation to New South Wales lasted until 1840. It began in Tasmania in 1803 and ended in 1852. To Western Australia, where it began in 1850, it ended in 1868.

For George and many other convicts, this strange new land Australia was to offer far more opportunity and a far better way of life than what they could have hoped to achieve had they stayed back home in England.

No one had prepared George for the shock he received on first sight of Regentville. Standing at the ornate gates at the entrance to the property, he could see a magnificent mansion in the distance. He was astonished at what his eyes saw. Miles from any town was this incredible building surrounded by miles and miles of open countryside. Well, not quite that open, perhaps, as George could see vineyards stretching in one direction and fruit trees in the opposite direction. Beyond the fruit trees appeared to be fields of wheat, and beyond the grapevines sheep were grazing.

Up the long carriageway his dusty entourage travelled, finally rounding the fountain in the front courtyard. His guard jumped down and marched up to the wide veranda where a gentleman was sitting in a small rocking chair. Sir John Jamison was not home but this was his half-brother Thomas, and together with the guard he came forward to look George over. "How long have you been a butcher, Mr. Dent?" he asked.

"Seven years, sir, save for one served as a green grocer."

"Have you worked with fowl as well as animals?"

"Yes sir. Chickens, ducks, geese, pigeons, and quail."

"What about rabbits?"

"Rabbits and hares both, sir."

"But no kangaroos yet I imagine?"

"No sir, not yet." George smiled.

"Lamb, mutton, beef, ham, and pork?"

"All of them, sir."

"Fish?"

"Well, that was generally the purview of the fishmongers, sir, but now and then we handled catfish and trout from the inland lakes and rivers for special customers."

"OK, it sounds like you have lots of experience, which we need. The last head butcher chap walked off two months ago and the two apprentices here are lacking in knowledge. Guard, thank you for bringing Mr. Dent all this way. If you'll go left around the house to the stables I'll arrange food and drink for you and your horse." Turning towards George, he stated, "Mr. Dent, I'll be back shortly to show you to your quarters, talk to you about an allowance and other arrangements, and give you a tour of the butchery. Please wait here."

George felt like pinching himself to check if this was all real. No guard, no orders or commands, someone had said 'please,' he was to get an 'allowance', and apprentices would work for him? And he was to work for the wealthy owner of this incredible mansion? It wasn't even a week ago that he had been housed in the stinking hold of a convict ship along with two hundred despairing and often desperate men, guarded day and night, seeing the sky once every few days for at most an hour at a time, and eating whatever swill the cook offered. This already felt like freedom. He wondered what more could be involved.

He strolled to the gardens by the fountain and admired the healthy rose bushes which he imagined were full of blooms in summer. Come to think of it, he hadn't seen flowers outside of those in the markets for years. Was this truly real? He turned back and saw a maid beckoning him. Good heavens, she had on a starched uniform, and she was both young and pretty. How long since he'd seen any woman? And now this one was signaling to him.

"Mr. Dent, if you'll come through to the kitchen there's a sandwich and some ale waiting for you. The manager was called away but said you might be hungry and thirsty. This way, please."

Another 'please,' and a sweet girl had called him by name? This was overwhelming, but the sandwich and beer tasted wonderful and he thanked the maid profusely. Out at the fountain again, he scooped fresh water in his hands, splashed his face, and slicked back his hair. He saw his reflection for the first time since robbing the store and was startled to see sunken eyes, and a narrowing of the face and accentuated eyebrows. He'd never had much facial hair, even as a lad growing up, and only had a mild stubble after his last shave on the boat perhaps a month ago. Maybe out here, he thought, it wouldn't take too long to regain his looks and the body he once had. That would really be something.

He looked up upon hearing the sound of crunching gravel as the manager returned. "Let's go, Mr. Dent, I'll show you around."

Not that life was easy as a butcher on the estate, for George not only had to provide meat for the mansion's residents but also the hundred-plus convicts, even though they got small rations of second-choice offerings. It was hard work, but George had never shied away from such, and over time, working primarily outdoors, he developed the typical sunburnt colour of first- and second-generation Australian whites, and regained the fitness he'd acquired when butchering and boxing for a living back in London. Unlike most convicts on the estate George was a constant visitor to the mansion, in working to meet the cook's interests for servings at both regular and special meals. He got to know all the kitchen help and many of the Jamison family through his frequent communication. Eventually he achieved a superior position of trust due to his honest, open nature, and willingness to help out and do good wherever he could. He strove daily to live up to his father's advice.

15. Heydays

The 1830s were the heydays of Sir John's life at Regentville. Whether measured in social engagements, political and judicial appointments, society presidencies, assigned convicts, land acreages, or animal herds, his worth was unmatchable. He had friends in high places all the way up to the governorship, he held influential positions in a variety of clubs and groups, well over one hundred convicts were assigned to him, and his land holdings were measured in tens of thousands of acres. Even smaller, non-political ventures were of importance for he was a member of the first committee to administer the Australian Museum and was involved with the management of the Botanical Gardens. On the family front, another daughter, Rebecca Marie, was born to Mary in 1833, and now there were six youngsters demanding attention in the dwelling.

Sir John became popular with the common man through his fights for their rights, and his mind and practices were constantly geared to having Australia become regarded as a respected country in its own right, moving beyond its penal colony heritage. With increasing exports of fine wool, and expanding supplies of beef, lamb, pork, and mutton to the slaughterhouses, he certainly grew richer, with beneficiaries in the family and across the economy. Regentville by now was well known, but Sir John kept on buying up neighbouring properties, so that his mansion became an even more meaningful dwelling for miles in many directions.

Not all visitors to Regentville were as impressed as he would have liked, however. Richard Bourke, son of Governor Bourke, for one, complained in October 1832 that the house had

"'with singular awkwardness been placed completely out of sight of the beautiful River Nepean,' that it was 'as uncomfortable as one would [expect] from a Sailor and a Bachelor,' and that 'the bugs bit so dreadfully last night that I made interest with Dolly the housemaid & was allowed to sleep on the drawing room sofa'."

For some, like Richard Bourke, the setting was so different from the moors and the stone-built fences of small English fields that they simple couldn't accept the dichotomy. Others, like Sarah Mathew, were spared any acquaintance with the bugs by merely observing the house as she travelled along the adjacent Mulgoa Road on 5 December 1833, thinking that Regentville was: "a handsome stone edifice, with a fine Porticoe, and balcony above it, the latter is quite a novelty here, and with its iron railing has quite an English look." Sir John never tired of showing off his grand rural mansion and worried none about any criticism.

Sir John still dealt with convicts stealing various farm implements and even cattle, and his overseers occasionally had to intervene in fights between Irish and English convicts at their camp, but on the whole the estate was well managed and highly productive in its agricultural output.

In November an ugly incident occurred at Sir John's northern property *Towardi* on the Peel River. Thomas Breechford and John Taylor were two convicts assigned to Sir John to help manage the sheep and cattle on the station. A third man, Farley, who had recently received his pardon and was free, shared the same hut. He and Breechford, returning from overnight shepherd duty one morning, found Taylor had been killed. Four natives chased Breechford away and two ran after Farley, who made it safely to a neighbouring property. There he recruited several men, who returned to Sir John's properties with guns. The aborigines had fled but the men found Taylor in a water hole, about forty yards from the hut, stripped naked. His abdomen had been cut open, and his brains beaten out. As well, a number of wounds had also been inflicted on various parts of the body, and one of his ears cut off by the savages.

On checking the hut Farley was able to determine that a number of items, including quantities of food and tobacco, arms, powder and shot, cooking utensils, apparel, and tools had been taken. His companion, Breechford, was found four days later about half a mile from the hut with his throat cut, head scalped, and several spear wounds in the back. The camp horse was found nearby, having apparently been used to carry off all the items. The police refused to investigate on the grounds that this property was at the fringes of the interior and therefore prone to unreasonable risk. Suspicion arose that perhaps a white man had been involved to some extent since many of the items that were stolen were beyond what natives usually were interested in. And there was abundant knowledge that runaway convicts had been known in the past to hook up with select aboriginal groups and live with them. In any event, the murderers were never apprehended. In certain instances Sir John would get involved pursuing suspects, but often there was little he could do, beyond exercising the law to its fullest when metering out appropriate justice for such criminals.

Farley stayed in the vicinity, becoming the overseer on Sir John's very large *Boan Baa* property on the bank of the Namoi River. His days, however, were numbered, for in September 1834 William McDonald's gang of bushrangers invaded the station and stayed overnight in one of the huts. The next morning they took a quantity of flour, a brace of pistols, and a variety of other articles, together with two stock-horses, and went searching for an extra horse known to be stabled at another hut on the property occupied by Farley. Warned by a fellow servant, Farley fled on his horse to escape, but in crossing the river he was unfortunately drowned.

The full story of this incident and the end of McDonald and his companion Lynch was detailed in *The Australian* on 2 Jan 1835.

"We have much satisfaction in being enabled to publish the interesting account, with which we have been favoured by Sir John Jamison, of the final termination of the lawless career of McDonald, the bushranger, and the remnant of his gang.

To the Hon. The Colonial Secretary
    Sir, - Many misrepresentations having gone abroad respecting the motives and the manner in which my assigned servants (Biddles and Archer) shot the two atrocious bushrangers M'Donald and Lynch, at my cattle station situate on the Nomoie River, I considered it only an act of justice to those brave and faithful servants, to take their statements, on oath, of all that occurred during the first visit of M'Donald and his banditti to my station on the 15th of September

last, and M'Donald and Lynch's second and last visit on the 13th ultimo; I have now the honor to enclose those statements for His Excellency's information, which I trust will be sufficient to place the courageous and meritorious conduct of Biddles and Archer in their true character, and I feel confident that His Excellency will confer on those men the boon of liberty and pecuniary reward promised in the Gazette of July last, to which they have so well founded a claim. I must next beg leave to bring under His Excellency's favourable consideration the conduct of Patrick Tye, a ticket of leave holder for upwards of six years, who in his position of stockkeeper to Mr Edward Cox, has (I am informed) apprehended within a few years twenty-eight bushrangers, some of them at much risk of his life, which appears to have brought upon him the hatred and intended vengeance of M'Donald and his gang. I will also take the liberty of recommending William Thomas, per ship Asia (10) my assigned servant and stockkeeper at the Nomoie, who, although unacquainted with the previously arranged determination of Biddles and Archer to oppose M'Donald and his gang, as soon as he saw what was going on ran with a loaded musket to attack Lynch, who at that moment received his death wound from Archer. I most anxiously hope that the destruction of these desperate characters by their fellow prisoners will operate more powerfully in deterring others from a similar lawless course of life, and will prove more discouraging to bushrangers, than if they had been taken by the constituted Authorities, and expiated their crimes on the gallows. Notwithstanding the local knowledge of M'Donald and his gang, enabled them to escape the vigilance of the mounted police for a few months, still their existence appears to have been that of wretchedness and fearful alarm for their safety. M'Donald and Lynch were absent from my station eight weeks and three days, and from their expectation that the mounted police would closely follow their track, their progress down the river must have been rapid, and the distance they penetrated into the interior very considerable. They described with terror to Thomas the great number, gigantic stature (seven feet in height) and ferocity of the native blacks, who they said threw the spear from the hand by its centre, and at first from such a distance as to penetrate but little deeper than the skin of their horses, but that afterwards they became so bold as to seize and pull round their horses by the tails, and added that the weather was so wet during the attack, that their firearms would not go off; for their protection, from the above statement, and the anxiety with which M'Donald and Lynch enquired of Thomas if he had seen any of their horses returning that way, especially a grey mare of Crawford's, it may reasonably be inferred, that the report is true which Nutty, the Nomoie chief received from the native blacks, viz. that one of the gang of white robbers had been shot by their own party, and two tumbled down (killed) by the natives, which would account for the destruction of the whole of M'Donald's party, which never exceeded five. Although M'Donald and Lynch's statement of the magnitude of the river and country they passed through, and the occurrences during their journey, may not be altogether correct, still it is sufficiently interesting to send an expedition to explore and ascertain the real character of the country they passed through, as the latter must be richly pastural from the good condition their horses were in, after so much fatigue. I feel confident that when the meritorious conduct of Biddles and Archer is generally known that many Colonists will cheerfully subscribe a small sum to afford these brave men the means of establishing themselves as free Colonists, and as an approval of their fidelity, and an encouragement to other assigned servants to protect their employers' property, as these men have done.

I have the honor to be, Sir,
Your most obedient humble Servant,
JOHN JAMISON

George Biddles, aged 32 years, per ship Asia under sentence of transportation for fourteen years, a native of Leicester, in Leicestershire, and formerly a marine in his Majesty's naval service. I landed in this Colony on the 26th of June, 1833, and was assigned to the service of Sir John Jamison in March last; I proceeded to Capita, to his new stock run, situate at the Namoie River, about eight miles below Barber's stock yard, and upwards of three hundred from Regent Ville, in a North West direction. On the 15th of September last, six men mounted, and in appearance like police men, with tether ropes and three pack horses, rode up to the hut in the dusk of the evening; Archer and Taylor, fellow servants, were in the hut with me; the six strangers alighted, being five white men and one aboriginal native, who appeared forced to accompany them as a guide, two went to tether their horses, the other three entered the hut, demanded the firearms, and took five unloaded muskets, and a brace of pistols, which they placed outside the door, they next searched our hut, and secured the flour, meat and cake. The man whom they repeatedly afterwards called Joe Lynch ... was a tall thin man, about six feet high, fair hair, and an effeminate voice, and apparently about five or six and twenty years of age; he wore a pair of black trousers, buttoned up the front, a fancy coloured shirt, a fustian shooting jacket, and a muslin cravat, a pair of half boots, and a straw hat; the shirt and trousers he boasted of having taken from Mr Robertson. They all assembled at tea, and assisted themselves to our cake and meat; after which, they brought in their bags from the pack horses, and commenced dividing the powder and shot, of which they appeared to have a considerable quantity. They all called M'Donald by name, whom they seemed to acknowledge as their chief; he was about five feet seven inches in height, dark complexion, black hair and whiskers, a scar on his nose, and (I think) slightly pockmarked, stout made, and about six and forty years of age, wore at this time a blue jacket, blue waistcoat, duck trousers, a pair of laced half boots, cut in several places, and a straw hat. ... I had some conversation with M'Donald during the night; he related the sundry robberies he had committed, and boasted the most of all in having wounded a police man who had charge of one of his party whom they captured; he told me he came to the Colony in the same ship as myself the first time she came; he further stated, that he had held the indulgence of a ticket of leave and lost it; I recommended him to give himself up to the law, he said no, I know my doom if taken, I will therefore endeavour to get out of the country, which I shall try to do in following the river. He added, that the police could not be more than a day or two behind, and desired me to tell Sergeant Temple that M'Donald and his mob had gone down the river, and that they would leave track enough for them. ... From their hatred to Patrick Tye, Mr Edward Cox's stockman, they were going to shoot his stock horse which they had with them, I begged them not to shoot the horse, in consequence of which they left him with us, being unserviceable to them, but stated if they found Patrick Tye at home when they went to his station, they would have punished him with 50 lashes each man, and then have shot him; they acknowledged they had taken all his arms, clothing, and ammunition, destroyed his provisions, and turned their horses to eat his wheat, and what the horses did not eat they threw about the bush; their hatred and vengeance against Patrick Tye was from his constant pursuit and capture of bushrangers in that quarter; after leaving the hut they went in quest of a mare in charge of a free man named Farley, who was fencing down the river, in the employment of Sir John Jamison; Taylor and Archer made the near cut to where Farley was at work, and informed him that the bushrangers were coming. Farley instantly mounted the mare, and attempted to swim the river, but the stream swept him off the mare and he was unfortunately drowned; four days after they left the station, one of the stock horses called Ball which they took away, returned with a piece of rope on his neck apparently having broken his tether.

... On Tuesday, at dusk in the evening of the 18th November last, as I looked from the hut door, I saw two armed men mounted, accompanied by two of Sir John's assigned servants of the names of Thomas, and Cooper, from the lower station, and as they drew near, ascertained them to be M'Donald and Lynch. ... M'Donald came into the hut and said, has Sir John sent you any more flour? Archer said yes; he said we will not distress you much this time, I shall only take away a little flour, and that horse in the stockyard; Archer said no, I'll be d___ if you take away any more horses, nor that one you have; Archer got up to go, his object being to collect people to assist in apprehending M'Donald and Lynch, and said, that he expected a man of their's had been waiting a day or two at Liverpool Plains with cattle; 'Little Jemmy' also said he must go, as he was going to assist; M'Donald directed Archer to remain, as he wanted him to go with him in the morning to Patrick Tye's, Archer said, for what? He said, he wanted to read Patrick Tye a lecture and give him a few pills; Archer said, that's a pretty thing to want me to go and see shot the best friend that I have got on the river, I would sooner be shot myself; M'Donald then told him that he had got that which would compel him to go; I had placed myself at the store door and covered five muskets, three of which were loaded; M'Donald had only a part of a hat on his head, and said, I must have one of you chaps hats, and a pair of boots, Archer said, I have no hat but the one on my head, or any opportunity of getting another; M'Donald said, the straw is coming in, you can soon make yourself another, I said Mac I don't think you will take that or anything else from this place anymore; Mac and myself got to words, he became much irritated, I said, there is nothing here but what belongs to my master; M'Donald said, Oh! You are one of the good men, I still told him he should have nothing, he said, Oh! d___ you, I'll have none of your bounce, he then placed his hand on the stock of his pistol from his belt, he was standing against the table about four or five yards off, with his side to me, making exertions to get his pistol from his left side, and rather turned his head with his hand, which brought the back part of his head to front me, and when in the act of drawing his pistol, I quickly snatched up the loaded I had my hand concealed on, and instantly fired and shot the top of his skull off, when he fell and died without a struggle, or even moved. ...

(signed) George Biddles

James Archer, aged 27 years, per ship Lord Melville, under sentence of transportation for fourteen years, a native of Bishops Storford, Essex, and an assigned servant of Sir John Jamison since his arrival in the Colony (1829), deposeth that he was present during both of M'Donald's and Lynch's visits to the hut at the Nomoie, and that the above statement is correct.

James Archer X his mark"

Not all was pleasurable in Sir John's world.

In the same month that Farley died on Sir John's property, Sir Edward Lytton Bulwer, M.P., wrote from England to the newspapers that the Australian situation was not well understood in London. He suggested that an organised association should be formed, and that it should appoint a parliamentary agent for New South Wales. As a result, the Australian Patriotic Association was created in 1835. Among the group's most notable leaders were W.C. Wentworth, the son of a convict woman and the publisher of the influential newspaper *The Australian*; Sir John, who became the association's president, and William Bland, a prominent emancipist doctor. The group sought a grant of representative government to the colony from the British House of Commons, standing as a champion of the rights of the less well-to-do and of former convicts. The group had representatives in England to put their case before the British government, which was then considering a new constitution for New South Wales. Their efforts aided significantly in the passage of the Constitution Act of 1842 and the incorporation of the city of Sydney as a municipality with a broadly based franchise. With its goals achieved, the APA disbanded in 1842.

Dr. William Bland was an unusual character with a matching unusual history. He was born in London, the second son of an obstetrician. In January 1809, he became a surgeon 5th grade aboard HM sloop *Hesper*. Onboard the ship in Bombay, India, he was involved in a wardroom argument with Robert Case, the purser. In the duel, which took place on 7 April 1813, Bland killed Case. He was convicted of manslaughter and transported to Van

Diemen's Land with a sentence of seven years transportation. While at Castle Hill gaol in Sydney he received a pardon 27 January 1815.

In 1818 he was gaoled at Parramatta for twelve months for writing satirical pieces criticising Governor Macquarie's treatment of farmers and making fun of his desire to have his name on foundation stones. Upon his release, the good side of the man shone through as he took up medical practice again and actively participated in public interests and causes. He was involved in establishing the Sydney Free Grammar School in 1825, serving as treasurer and president in later years. In 1830 he actively opposed attempts to alienate large areas of crown land, and in 1831 joined the committee of the Australian Landowners Association to fight the Ripon land regulations. He and Sir John were to serve together in multiple associations over the years. Much, much later in history, Dr. Bland's contributions to Australian medicine were recognized in the naming of a building after him located opposite Sydney Hospital in Macquarie Street, Sydney.

The mixture of skills in the convicts serving at Regentville was emulated nowhere else in the country. By 1835 Sir John had in his employ a parade of butchers, bakers, farriers, blacksmiths, coachmen, millwrights, tailors, horsebreakers, gardeners, grooms, shoemakers, cooks, butlers, coopers, carpenters, harness makers, wheelwrights, shepherds, overseers, engineers, dairymen, seedsmen, cattle handlers, vintners, arborists, nannies, and governesses. Plus a number of maids serving a variety of functions in and around the house itself. The range of skills and experience needed on the estate widened as Sir John's holdings in the vicinity grew. In the first month of the year he even added a wool comber and a maltster. His acquisition of talent seemed to never cease.

Sir John worked hard at both running his properties and managing the various agricultural pursuits thereon, in addition to tirelessly working to improve the prosperity of the country at large. He worked hard and played hard, as the saying goes, still flirting and indulging himself at every second opportunity. Busy as he was, he loved to celebrate life, and as an unpublicised early recognition of his looming sixtieth birthday a year away, he planned an innovative Fancy Dress Ball to which the aristocracy of the colony would be invited.

Consequently, on Thursday 12 March 1835, one of the most elaborate social events ever to be held in or outside Sydney took place at Sir John's country home. There was no question that the fete, or ball, was a smashing success. Over the following days the Sydney newspapers wrote up eloquent descriptions of the gala. From the *Sydney Herald* on 16 March came the following summary:

THE FETE AT REGENTVILLE.
We hope the worthy Knight will have succeeded in attaining one of his main objects in giving his elegant fete -which was to promote social intercourse and enjoyment among the respectable and wealthy colonists.

"An entertainment on a very splendid and extensive scale was given during the week at RegentVille, the estate of Sir John Jamison, but which through the heavy rains that set in on Wednesday last, deranged both those plans of Sir John and his visitors. Upwards of five hundred invitations were sent round to families of respectability in the Colony, and Thursday was the day named for the fete, Major England of the 50th Regiment, and Captain Collins from India, accepting the office of Stewards upon the occasion.

For the last fortnight a great number of workmen were employed making preparations to accommodate the visitors, and preparing the feast. On the lawn in front of Sir John's house, was erected a large hall-room, capable of holding all that were invited, round which were a number of tents, intended as dressing places for the gentlemen, the house being set apart for the ladies. A number of families left Sydney for RegentVille, on Wednesday, but the rain falling in such torrents, caused some to put back, and others to take refuge in the first house they could reach. On Thursday the weather continued the same; and, notwithstanding, numbers of families were seen travelling to the centre of attraction, and about noon, the visitors began to arrive at RegentVille, their vehicles and servants presenting rather droll spectacles from the deplorable state of the roads.

At about five o'clock in the afternoon, about one hundred persons sat down to a dinner which comprised all the delicacies of the country. During the dinner, a great many men were employed in illuminating the ballroom and the house, the former being decorated with lamps in festoons, the lower end presenting a sort of theatre, with a scene of a waterfall, also an Australian scene, which represented a Currency lad and lass, with kangaroos in the back ground; over the orchestra the word "Welcome," in lamps, so as to meet the eye of the visitor as he entered the room, and a great quantity of evergreens and fruit tastefully placed about the ballroom.

On the front of the house were the words "Ventis Secundis," the verandah being also illuminated with lamps, the whole of which presenting a scene never before witnessed in the Australian bush. At about nine o'clock most of the company that could be expected in such disagreeable weather having arrived, some of the gentlemen of the 17th Regt. led the way to the ballroom, and were followed by the rest of the company, the majority of whom entered in fancy dresses of the most costly description.

The bands of the 17th and 4th Regiments being in attendance, the party immediately commenced dancing, Mr. Cavendish being the conductor of the ceremonies. At this time the ballroom presented a very animated scene, and contained about two hundred persons, splendidly dressed in the costumes of various nations—Greeks, Turks, Swedes, Normans, Spaniards, Frenchmen, Indian, Dutch, Flemings, &c. The dancing continued until morning, when the company retired to the supper table, which was arranged under the verandah of the house. After supper, the cloth being removed, several toasts were given, and on the health of Sir John Jamison being drank, the worthy Knight rose and delivered a neat and most appropriate speech, which was followed by a number of other toasts and speeches. On returning to the ballroom, the company kept on "the light fantastic toe," until near daylight, when the amusements were concluded by a splendid display of fireworks.

A party of vocalists from Sydney were in attendance for the purpose of giving a Concert, but the rain having altered the arrangements of the evening, the idea of a Concert was given up. During the Ball, two circumstances occurred which somewhat disturbed the amusements of the evening; the first was, that of the stables unfortunately catching fire through the carelessness of a drunken groom, and which was not extinguished without much trouble. A man and three horses were considerably injured by the accident. The other circumstance was that of a man intruding himself into the ballroom in the dress of lawyer hue, who was on discovery turned out.

Extra information from a second account added that:

The worthy Knight was indefatigable in his attention to the company. It is to be hoped that the universal satisfaction expressed, will recompense him for the excess of trouble he must have taken in the arrangement of a far more splendid thing than had hitherto been seen in the Colony. As a first fancy ball, it is perhaps singular, though true, that there was really no one thing to find fault with. The characters were generally excellent—mostly very appropriate, and many of the costumes highly rich and elegant—nothing tawdry —no making up of scraps. The Solicitor General [Jno Hubert Plunkett] added exceedingly to the liveliness of the scene, by the vivacity with which he enacted his character.

A third description in *The Australian* on 17 March applied delightful humour where appropriate, in concluding:

It is impossible to give an adequate description of the scene — but it was universally agreed that, a gayer or more brilliant assemblage had never been witnessed; at least two thirds of, the company were in fancy dresses of the gayest description; and, the room altogether presented more the appearance of a gala in fairy land, than of a company of sober, modern, matter of fact ladies and gentlemen. The dresses are too numerous to mention — and the following cannot therefore pretend to be a correct list; as far however as our memory serves us we shall give them...

There were two or three Queen Elizabeths, in an appropriate but not very becoming costume — Mrs. C. Chambers, and Mrs. Bell, - ; Mrs. Captain Faunce as *Titania*, and Mrs, Collins as *Queen Mab* ; three Miss Wilsons — one as a *Spanish*, another as a *Norman Lady*, and the third looking the very picture of a Nun for whom one would scale a convent wall and defy the Inquisition; Miss Plunkett as Flora McIvor, to the life; Miss Kemp as a *French* and Miss Amy Kemp as a *Swiss Peasant* (well worth crossing the Alps or ascending Mont Blanc to look at;) Mrs. E. Deas Thompson as an *Indian Princess*; Mrs. Wilson as '*La Suisse au bord du lac;* " Miss Manning as a *French Flower Girl*; the Miss Kirks in *French Dresses*; Miss Allan in the *Stuart Plaid*; the Miss Gibbs as *Swiss Peasants*; the Miss Bells as *Flower Girls*; Miss Savage as a *Norman Lady*; Miss Carter as the same; Mrs. Plunkett ditto.

Sir J. Jamison himself was in a splendid *Court Dress* of the present reign, and we were happy to see, in the highest health and. spirits ; Major England as a *Spanish Muleteer*, and Captain Collins as a *Spanish Grandee* ; Colonel Wilson in a *South American Uniform*, looking like the picture of George the Fourth ; Major Gibbs as a *Dandy of King Henry's Reign*; Mr. Rankin as a *Nondescript* ; Mr. Ebden, Mr. Driscol and Mr. Lawson, as *Bandits*; Mr. Brennard as the *Huntsman in Der Freischutz* ; Mr. Park as a *Knight of St. John*, mysterious and unintelligible, as a Free Mason should be; Dr. Kenny, like a glass of *"Half-and-half,"* one side representing a soldier, and the other a civilian; Mr. K. Deas Thompson as a *Persian Vakheel*; Mr. Holden something of the same kind; Mr. Gisborne as *Douglas in the Abbott*; Mr. Hardy as *Pluto*; two Faunces — the Captain as a *Portuguese Muleteer*; the other. as the very best *Broom Girl* that ever handled her brush in a ball-room; Mr. Markham an excellent *Paul Pry*; Mr. Plunkett as an *Irish Fidler* was inimitable; two McLeays, one as a *Highlander*, the other as a *Spanish Grandee*; Lieutenant Campbell; Mr. Andrew Allan, and Mr. McIntyre in *Highland Dresses*; Mr. Riley as a *German Student*; Mr. Bell and Messrs. Blaxland as *Bandits*; Dr. Lewis as a *Greek*; Mr. C. Chambers as *"My Pretty Page"*; Mr. Riddell, as one of the *Royal Archers*; Mr. Ryder, *Old Court Dress*; Mr. Ainslie *21st French Hussars*; Mr. Lamotte, *2lst National Guards*.

The number of guests was above 300 — among whom, were to be found, most of the principal persons in the Colony. Dancing was kept up with great spirit till past two o'clock, when supper was announced; there was sitting room for nearly all the visitors' at once, and the few who were shut out probably fared as well as their neighbours when they at last succeeded. The supper was of the most costly and elegant description, and reflects 'infinite credit upon Dunsdon, the confectioner, who had the superintendence of it; all sorts of eatables, and oceans of wines from Champagne to humble Port, fruit, confectionery, of all sorts, to be eaten and to be looked at, covered the tables; how the thing could have been done so well at such a distance from Sydney, is a puzzle.

After supper dancing recommenced, and was kept up till long after daylight had opened upon the scene; but alas all things must have an end — a Fancy Ball must break up as well as a Ministry, and by six o'clock the ladies had retired, and the gentlemen dispersed to bewail their departure and to undress; mattresses were spread on the floors for those who chose to sleep, and wine and wassail for not a few who preferred them. At twelve o'clock the same morning breakfast was provided, and the guests re-assembled; the meal was ended and — Farewell to RegentVille.

Altogether the whole affair went off in the most satisfactory manner; the excellence of the arrangements — the care and attention of the managers, — the liberal and unsparing hand with which everything was provided, — and the nature of 'the party, caused it to be as sumptuous and splendid an entertainment as was ever given.

This Ball will form an era in the history of New South Wales; people at home will begin to think that New South Wales is after all, not such a very objectionable spot to reside in, and here events will recollected by this occurrence, just as an old woman starts her tales from 'my last illness', and an old man from the loss of his last tooth; independently of the good effect it is likely to have in bringing people to be sociable and hospitable, it has given no slight spur to trade in various branches; the tailors, milliners, and drapers have reaped a good harvest— as well as the inn keepers, housekeepers, &c.

A hope was expressed after supper, in giving the health of. the Founder of the Feast, that "this would not be the last in the Colony" — we trust not— though it cannot be expected that many such will follow; they are only a favored few who have the means at their command — and, of these, many would look at seven or eight hundred pounds a long time before they would take less than 10 per cent for it, and many more would (to use the energetic language of the Colonist), "look a d— d sight longer at it" before they gave it up to the promotion of the interests or the happiness of the Colonists.

As a Ball it was decidedly gayer than most provincial balls of the same description at home; there the majority go in Court dresses, or in plain red coats, the different costumes being left to the ladies.

A ridiculous circumstance occurred in the appearance, about twelve o'clock, of a very strangely dressed figure with large grey whiskers — everybody was wondering who he was, when he was recognised by Mr. Rankin as a Mr. Barsden, who had been some short time previously tried for cattle stealing! He was immediately kicked out, and taken by the constables in his fancy dress to enlighten the minds of the inhabitants of Penrith watch-house.

Sir John's incredible generosity and the unconditional nature of his invitations to the event were recognized throughout the colony, as evidenced in the newspaper article above. In his welcoming speech Sir John told his friends and acquaintances that he experienced no small degree of pride in being the first to establish a form of entertainment that must inevitable bind society together, and which perhaps might cause friendship and good feeling where formerly animosity and hatred had existed. He hoped many of those would return to Regentville as visitors in the years to come. Undisputedly, a man of the ages.

Even while the fancy dress ball was under way Sir John and graziers everywhere were facing a serious problem. Sheep were suffering from a problem called 'black disease', which was a bacterial liver disease like hepatitis. It decimated flocks, and although offering salt blocks helped, many growers lost a lot of money. The lack of water caused by the following drought sustained the problem for several years. In partial early response the Australian Agricultural Company formed in January 1836 and Sir John generously donated large quantities of wine for the opening ceremony at Landsdowne bridge on George's River.

Among Sir John's closer friends was a free settler named Robert Dulhunty. The well-read son of a medical doctor, Dulhunty had arrived in Sydney in 1824 whence he immediately applied for, and was granted, two thousand acres at Cullen Bullen, and assigned six convict servants. Cullen Bullen was a little over twenty-five miles north northwest of Mt. Victoria and offered prime grazing land. Sir John held acreage there and, as neighbours, the men cultivated their herds and grew rich together. Dulhunty rose through the ranks of colonial society. With a zeal for exploration he and a team of forty aborigines forged a path over two hundred and fifty miles northwest of Sydney to the interior. He liked the discovered area so much that in 1832 he took up land on the Macquarie River at a place there later named Dubbo.

In 1836 Dulhunty became a founding member of Sydney's elite Australian Club, the first meeting of which was held in October 1836. The club's initial eighty-six members included other such prominent citizens as W.C. Wentworth, Sir John Jamison,

Captain John Piper, Dr William Bland, Major Edmund Lockyer, James Macarthur, William Lithgow, and John Blaxland.

A year later at St. James Church of England in Sydney , Dulhunty married Eliza Gibbes, daughter of Major John Gibbes, the Collector of Customs. Dulhunty and his wife held their wedding party on Sydney's Point Piper, where the Gibbes family lived. They honeymooned, however, at Sir John's Regentville mansion. Major Gibbes had married Elizabeth Davis, the daughter of a clergyman, at the 17th-century Church of St Andrew, Holborn, in London in 1814. He migrated to Australia in 1834 along with his eight children. Eliza was his first daughter.

Somewhat coincidentally, but more likely the result of neighbourly propinquity, Sir John's first surviving daughter, Harriet, was betrothed to the major's second son, William John. They were also married in St. James Church, later, Thursday 20 April, making 1837 a banner year for the Gibbes family, and the bonding between the Jamisons and Gibbes clans.

For Sir John, the crowning glory of the year was when he took his seat in the Legislative Assembly—something he had desired for years. A happier man would have been hard to find.

16. *In the Eye of the Beholder*

As the penal colony slowly moved forward in its transition to a civilized state, the British population started to show more interest in the antipodean country. Convicts were still being sent there, but in the press the names of new towns kept emerging, along with courageous tales of discovery. The imports of much finer wool than available from the continent, stories of the strange native animals and birds, along with information about the ever-present sunshine, deep harbours, and fertile grazing and farming land started to change people's perceptions, and the emigration of free settlers increased. It also happened that the NSW government and its English governorship wanted to attract more of the same and a bounty scheme was established to bring able-bodied families to the new land.

James Maclehose saw an opportunity and started collecting information on the positive qualities of the colony. He turned these into a travel advisory book, designed to help attract Britons to Australia. His *Picture of Sydney and Strangers' Guide in NSW for 1839* was very well done as it contained "forty four engravings of the public buildings and picturesque land and water views in and near Sydney." As well there was a fold-out map of the Town of Sydney in 1837 with street and building names shown. As a first tourist guide to Sydney it was an excellent offering, even including realistic "Hints to Immigrants" pondering a move across the oceans. While a few political remarks on government idiosyncrasies were included, in general it painted a very positive advertisement for those inclined to a little adventure. Among its descriptions of public and private buildings of note was a picture and description of Regentville.

This splendid mansion, vying in magnificence of structure with the princely residences of some of the nobility of Great Britain, is situated about 35 miles from Sydney and a quarter hour's ride of Penrith. The wealthy founder of this beautiful edifice is Sir John Jamison, a member of the Legislative Council, and one of the oldest and most respected of the colonists of New South Wales.

The beauty of the surrounding scenery, being situated at the foot of the Blue Mountains, cannot fail of riveting the attention of the stranger on first beholding "Regentville" - heightened, as it is, by a well-cultivated garden and a well laid-out park, and splendid agricultural improvements.

On this valuable estate, also, there is the largest vineyard in the colony; and it is to the patriotic exertions of Sir John Jamison that Australia is indebted for the early manufacture of wine - some of the examples of which have been of the very finest quality. It is to be hoped that others of the wealthy class will follow his meritorious example in this particular, by which means the unwholesome, as well as pernicious, liquid imported into New South Wales as "Cape Wine" will, for the future, cease to be brought to our shores.

Maclehose's genteel treatment of all the buildings and other aspects of his guide prevented him from offering too elaborate a description of any one place, as he was very conscious not to offend anybody in his descriptions. In essence his book was a 'sales brochure' with enough appropriate information to titillate and provoke interest in its readers.

One of the more delicate but innovative components of Sir John's mansion was a 'multi-seat privy', certainly not an appropriate topic for the Sydney guide. Commonly, in the early 1800s, privies were simple outdoor shacks with a seat over a deep hole in the ground. At Regentville more comfort was offered. First, the privy was integrated within the basic design of the west wing. It had access from the courtyard for servants, as well as from outside the compound and, most importantly, from indoors, thereby avoiding trips in inclement weather for nature calls. Second, it was not a single commode, but due to an array of stalls, allowed private use by several people at the same time, if necessary.

The privy was located against the southern wall of the billiard room with drains directing roof run-off through the privy pit and into the main drain that carried water out of the courtyard. The system did not flush per se but avoided many of the less salubrious aspects of the usual privy design and arrangements that were standard at the time. It was decades later before water closets became a feature of upscale homes.

Mary Griffiths had given birth to Maria Matilda the year before the guide was printed, in 1838, so that now six children filled the mansion, since Harriet had married and moved away. Jane was fifteen, Mary thirteen, Robert ten, William eight, and Rebecca six. For any normal household this would have been quite a handful, but with lots of help that Sir John could afford it was less of an issue at Regentville. Mary was only thirty-nine years old, but Sir John was now sixty-three.

Living at Regentville in the second half of 1839 was a newly arrived immigrant named Henry Parkes and an infant named Thomas Bent, the former to become Premier of New South Wales and the latter Premier of Victoria. In England, Henry had set up in business for himself as a bone and ivory turner but was unsuccessful. He married Clarinda Varney and their first two children sadly died. They moved to London in the hope of finding work but eventually decided to immigrate to NSW. Clarinda's third baby was born on the ship a few days prior to arrival in Sydney in July. The family had precious little money, Henry had no job prospects in Sydney, and so they ventured westward like others before (and after) them, finally finding shelter at Regentville.

Henry was highly critical of Sir John's treatment of workmen. In a letter to friends in England in May 1840 he stated:

At length, being completely starved, I engaged as a common labourer with Sir John Jamison, Kt., M.C., to go 36 miles up the country. Sir John agreed to give me £25 for the year, with a ration and a half of food. This amounted to weekly: 10½ lb. beef, sometimes unfit to eat, 10½ lb. rice, 2 lb. sugar, ¼ tea inferior, ¼ soap, not enough to wash our hands, 2 figs tobacco, useless to me.

This was what we had to live upon, and not a leaf of vegetable or a drop of milk beyond this. For the first four months we had no other bed than a sheet of bark off a box tree, and an old door laid on two cross pieces of wood, covered over with a few articles of clothing. The hut appointed for us to live in was a very poor one. Morning sunshine, the noontide shower, and the white moon- light of midnight, gushed in upon us alike.

> You will perhaps, think, had you been with us you would have had a
> few vegetables at any rate, if you would have made a bit of a garden
> and cultivated them for yourself; but you would have done no such
> thing; the slave-masters of New South Wales require their servants
> to work for them from sunrise to sunset, and will not allow them to
> have gardens lest they should steal a half-hour's time to work them.

Compared to other stories of employee treatment this seems
quite contrary. Perhaps Henry felt he should have been accorded
prestigious treatment for some reason, although as he states, he
came as a beggar. Hours of work were regulated by the Crown and
labourers definitely had time to themselves. Tenants on the farm,
of which there were maybe twenty, were in a different class with
laid out plots of acreage growing produce essentially for Sir John.
But the labourer camp had mini gardens where vegetables were
grown, rights to tiny plots often being a source of conflict for camp
occupants. Apparently Henry also assumed he'd be granted an
elegant abode, but these were parceled out on the basis of
seniority and time of arrival, so he was at the bottom end of the
occupancy list. His letter sounds more like one of 'sour grapes'
than anything else.

Sir John was born in Ireland, but spent most of his early life in
England or on English ships. Many of the labourers he hired were
of Irish descent. Many were convicts, although later, more and
more were bounty-supported free settlers. John himself was
Anglican with his children baptised in that faith. Daughter Harriet
was married in St. James Church of England. But just as Sir John
supported workers regardless of nationality or criminal status, he
was also unbiased and indifferent with respect to their religion.

Workers themselves, however, were very conscious of their
religion. On a day-to-day basis Irish Catholics and Anglicans got on
well as this was before Irish religious troubles erupted later in the
century. They worked together, drank in the pubs together, sang
Gaelic songs together, and intermarried. Yet when they died their
announced preferences were to be buried alongside others of
their denomination. Recognizing this, and observing that an
increasing number of his workers were Irish, Sir John designated a

small hill on his property to be used as an Irish cemetery. The ground was consecrated by Archbishop Polding in 1839 and some Catholics were re-buried there subsequently. Sir John later donated the ground to the Catholic church and it remains in existence to this day.

Was this the same man accused of parsimonious treatment of his workers by Henry Parkes?

17. Irish Immigrants

Throughout 1840 and 1841 the rural expansion in New South Wales slowed dramatically. There was no single cause. Rather, a number of interconnected factors played into the timing of the resultant depression. The amount of free grazing land handed out by authorities declined, and on the world market the price of wool started falling. Financial difficulties in London slowed capital inflow, and the end of convict transportation to eastern Australia stalled the availability of inexpensive labour. Government revenues and expenditures in both England and Australia slowed significantly.

Labour-intensive pastoralism was the engine of the Australian economy, and unfortunately relatively little agricultural or manufacturing diversification had occurred over the years. Pastoralism generated more jobs in the commercial port cities in transport, warehousing, finance, construction, provisioning, and administration than on the inland frontier. Suddenly all the small enterprises in these industries were in jeopardy.

As with most depressions there was massive deflation. Retail prices and wages fell by a third to a half. The prices for sheep and cattle collapsed. The only thing of any value in sheep was their tallow fat, which was obtained by boiling them down in vast quantities. Workers were laid off and unemployment attended hundreds of families and bankrupted many businesses and trades people across the land.

As bad as it was, the situation hardly compared to the drastic condition of the Irish economy. Poverty was at a level there that Australian citizens would never see in their lifetimes. A report by Thomas Campbell Foster, written on 3rd September 1845 in *The Times* newspaper, summarized a previous visit to County Donegal. From Donegal town he:

> "proceeded to Glenties, a village which is the property of the Marquis of Conyngham. The whole of the country for many miles in the direction of Dungloe and beyond that town, in fact almost the whole barony of Boylagh belongs to this nobleman, together with the island of Arran on the west coast. Once in the course of his

lifetime, two years ago, the marquis visited his estate for a few days. His chief agent Mr. Benbow, usually comes once a year and the sub-agents visit the tenants every half year to collect the rents. At short periods of a few years the farms are visited to see what increases in rent they will bear and this is the extent of the acquaintance of the marquis with his tenants. This nobleman himself, bears the character of a 'kind-hearted, generous man, fond of yachting and amusement and having an excess of distaste for every kind of business trouble'. From one end of his large estate here to the other, nothing is to be found but poverty, misery, wretched cultivation and infinite subdivision of land. There are no gentry, no middle class, all are poor, wretchedly poor.

"Every shilling the tenants can raise from their half-cultivated land is paid in rent, whilst most people subsist for the most part on potatoes and water. Every rude effort that they make to increase the amount of their produce is followed immediately by raising their rents in proportion, as it were, to punish them for improving; they are, naturally enough, as discontented and full of complaints as they are wretched in their condition."

Foster reported in minute detail what he found when he visited some of the homes, if such they could be called, of the 'noble' marquis' tenants.

"Into the cottages I entered. They were stone-built and well roofed but the mud floor was uneven, damp and filthy. In one corner was a place for the pig, with a drain from it through the wall to carry off the liquid manure, like a stable. Two chairs, a bedstead of the rudest description, a cradle, a spinning wheel and an iron pot constituted the whole furniture. An inner room contained another rude bedstead; the mud floor was quite damp. In this room six children slept on loose hay, with one dirty blanket to cover them. The father, mother and an infant slept in the first room, also on loose hay, and with but one blanket on the bed. The children were running about as nearly naked as possible, dressed in the cast off rags of the father and mother; the father could not buy them clothes.

"The men assured me that their whole food was potatoes and if they had a penny to spare they bought salt or a few sprats, but very seldom these. Instead of buying salt they sometimes bought pepper and mixed it with the water they drank. This they called 'kitchin', it gave a flavour to their food."

Moving to Dungloe, a village sixteen miles further, direct north, also owned by the 'ever-caring' marquis, Foster again described:

"Filthy and wretched cottages housing not only pigs but calves and ducks dabbling in a pool of dirty water in a hole in the mud floor."

While his report was dated 1845, he knew the conditions had been worsening for years. At first as conditions deteriorated, families squabbled. Wives complained about not having enough food to feed children and themselves adequately; husbands complained about the extra hours they were required to work to bring in the same pennies. Frustration led to anger, and sometimes to shoving matches. There were stories from other villages where men had simply up and left and walked into a river and drowned themselves, which made things only worse for those left behind. Widowed wives retreated with children to parents' and sisters' and brothers' abodes, increasing the strain there. The cycle was vicious, with no winners other than the marquis. Villagers wondered at their plight. What was the purpose of going on? To see their children withering away, malnourished and disheartened? There were no easy answers.

For many, the conditions were too much to bear, and they sought to migrate elsewhere. The British had started the "Assisted Immigrant" Bounty scheme to Australia in 1836 for healthy citizens under forty years old. The reasons reflected a combination of events. Not only was there widespread rural poverty in Ireland, but a different form of poverty existed in England, Wales, and Scotland as well. There, the harsh conditions of the industrial cities also added to the misery. Migration to Australia became an attractive option for many, but few had the resources to pay for a berth even in steerage, which cost on the order of seventeen pounds.

Matthew and Ellen Bourke and their seven children had watched people join the emigration ranks for four years.

It was Matthew who finally brought the topic to a head. "As much as we have suffered here, Ellen, I don't think we are being fair to our children and ourselves. I try to be optimistic but I have run out of energy to be so. I cannot see things improving and we are living in a state that I never wanted for us. It is shameful, and I am embarrassed for us and our children. I have thought long and hard, and as much as the kinship in the village helps, I think we must leave. Others have set an example by emigrating, and the bounty men weave a tale that has promise, even given their hyperbole and ability to make everything seem positive. I cannot see it being worse than what we have now."

"I've had similar thoughts, Matthew, but wondered if you'd feel ill of me were I to voice them. I dread the thought of leaving our families, but worry about our future here. I will follow you anywhere, and if that's to be Australia, so be it. If it's to stay here, again so be it. You and the boys have the best chance at earning income and for me that should probably be our main concern, so that we earn enough to feed us all. Even though the eldest girls are also farm servants now, and Ann also brings in a little money as a child's maid, it's still not enough because we have more mouths to feed than others." She hesitated before continuing. "I do wish we had heard back directly from those who had gone to Australia before us instead of just from the bounty men and the town criers."

"Well, my love, if you are willing, I will add our names to the list of the next bounty man who comes by. It's our last chance, as once I turn forty years old next year I will no longer be eligible. I hate to leave, but life here is utterly miserable and I want better for all of us."

And thus it came to pass that in 1840 the Burkes of Drumcairn townland made the decision to seek a new and better life elsewhere, before it was too late to do so.

Neither parent, nor any of the children, had ever been on a ship before, and the brand new barque, the *Herald*, whose deck they stood on and whose rail they fearfully clutched, creaked and groaned continuously. Yet she hadn't even left the wharf. The temporary excitement and confidence they'd felt on first seeing her and noting her enormous size was gone. This was no longer a dream. Reality was upon them. They had walked fifty miles across country to the city of Londonderry. What on earth would it be like in the vast ocean waters they had to cross? More than three months at sea awaited them. There was no turning back now.

The noise level from the dock decreased as the last access gangplank was removed. Contrarily, on board, shouted commands and responses increased as sailors climbed into the rigging and the lines securing the ship to the dock were released and hauled aboard. Slowly, inexorably, the hull parted company with the pilings of the wharf. The gap between ship rail and shore widened, and at last Ellen released the pent-up anxiety she'd held inside, with giant sobs that racked her thin frame. Matthew dropped her hand and his comforting arm reached around her shoulders.

She raised her head skyward and whispered silently, "Lord, what have we done?"

Matthew gathered the brood close together and they knelt on the deck, where he offered a prayer. "May God hold us all gently in his palms, guide the captain and this ship safely to the new land, and bless all of us onboard in our quest to start a new life. We thank you, Lord, for your benevolence, and pray your forgiveness for past sins. Amen."

Few on board had acquaintances on the dock so the departure was eerily non-festive. Some desultory waves with handkerchiefs wiping away tears were the norm. Like the Burkes, most of the other passengers wondered what on earth was ahead. Those few souls left on shore shook their heads at the perceived bravery or foolishness of relatives and friends moving so far away. Not for them at all.

As the boat moved to midstream, more sails were unfurled, and the vessel made a pretty sight as she headed northward for the Irish Sea and the Atlantic beyond.

It was Saturday, 10 April, 1841.

Three months later, after an uneventful trip across the Atlantic and Indian Oceans, Captain Coubro sailed between the heads of Sydney Cove on Thursday 15 July. This was his fastest trip ever, completed in the amazingly short time of only one hundred and six days. Temporarily holding against the wind off the growing village of Manly, the *Herald* fired her welcome cannons. The deck rails were awash with passengers admiring the rocky shores, sandy beaches, and thick bushland on either side of the Cove. The outlook seemed appealing and not at all frightening. The harbour water stretched ahead, welcome and calm compared to the enormous seas they had come through.

Slowly, the pilot ship steered their sea-home to a central spot off the Quay. The rattle of the anchor chain pierced the hearts of three hundred and sixty-two immigrants standing on deck, but they cheered anyway, thankful to have arrived safely at last.

The promised land was before their eyes.

It took two days to land everyone ashore. Captain Coubro and Dr. Wark handed over their records to the immigration authorities and ship's agents. At least fifteen people had died along the way—one sailor, two emigrants, nine infants from teething and other complaints, two older girls from influenza, and one baby from causes unknown. One other baby born had survived. The authorities regretted the deaths but were pleased with the number of single females and the variety of trades the men brought with them. Sixty-seven men were agricultural workers, twenty were carpenters, five masons, eight shepherds, and one each a gardener, butcher, bricklayer, and ploughman.

But the illusion of the promised land eroded quickly as everyone learned that a depression was settling in in the country. A daunting welcome. It was a tedious and frustrating process to find work. It was the eldest Burke boys who found the first jobs working on a farm at Lane Cove on the north shore. (The spelling of the family name was changed from Bourke to Burke due to an error made by the Bounty man.) There was a small two-room shepherds' slab cottage on the property that served as the first Sydney abode for the family. It was highly inadequate, taking them back to facilities similar to what they had in Drumcairn. Suddenly, reminders of home were everywhere, blighting their expectations.

Sydney Cove was formed between two headlands—the low-lying one to the east called Benelong Point and that to the west, Dawes Point. The town itself covered one and a half miles due south, along the depression between Dawes Point and Benelong

Point, and included the hill behind Dawes Point, and the next deep bay called Darling Harbour. From beyond Farm Cove on the other side of town, there rose a hill in an area named Woolloomooloo after the aboriginal term *Wallamullah*, meaning 'place of plenty'. Several considerable country houses, looking as though they had just arrived from England, graced the district, but instead of trees on the hill there was only a giant windmill.

Elsewhere in town, major streets were wide and in good order. Standard-type cottages were of a good size, many with verandas around them, with few that did not have a small garden, some with English roses, in front. On Sundays, military bands played in the streets, or by the wharves, and there was little to convey the notion that this was indeed the capital of a penal colony, beyond the presence of the military garrison, the local prison, and chain gangs at work. At the Quay where passengers first set foot on Australian soil, a new circular wharf was being started at the eastern end of the cove. The Tank Stream poured water slowly into the harbour at the other end. Citizens were proud of the new gas lamps being placed in the main streets, as they added a factor of safety that all the women of the town liked. They still illuminated their private homes with cheaper oil lamps, however, rather than gas ones.

At Farm Cove, Macquarie Point provided a wonderful vista of the harbour with views both east and west. It was one of Matthew and Ellen's favorite stopping spots. With no job for either they were usually alone during the day. They spent much of the available time exploring the city. And with the available propinquity and absence of elder children they re-established the intimate physical contact which they'd chastely denied themselves on the voyage out. Fecund as she had been proven, Ellen knew she was pregnant five months after arrival, and in July of 1842 she gave birth to a son, David. Another mouth to feed, but loved by all.

It then became more important to find a bigger house, and fortunately Matthew found one in late spring of 1842 across the water at Hen and Chicken Bay. The family was not unhappy to leave Lane Cove, as vagrants, outcasts, and illicit grog-sellers, for whatever reason, had started to inhabit the area. In the *Sydney*

Gazette of February 25 1841, an article stated that Lane Cove was "the resort of disreputable people...as great a set of ruffians as the colony holds."

As the summer of early 1843 faded into autumn, less than six months after moving, Matthew called the family together one evening. In a rare emotional state he addressed his sons and daughters. "I want to thank you all from the bottom of my heart for the faith you've exhibited in your mother and me as we've made this enormous change in our lives coming here to Australia. You have put up with conditions only slightly better than what we had back home in Drumcairn, and that is unacceptable to me and your mother. We were led to believe things would be far different, and while we don't regret bringing you all here we wish life were easier. You have all been uncomplaining, and incredibly supportive and opportunistic, and for that we can only say thanks. I'm proud when neighbours, acquaintances, and employers speak positively of you all. But we think we can do better than our life here in this Bay. As you know, the newspapers are full of tales of opportunity west of Parramatta. And while no one can be certain of the future, there are enough positive tales from the mouths of travelers that we feel obliged to see what might be there for us.

"So once again we are going to journey on. It will be hard because we don't have a lot of money, but the Lord has looked after us before and we feel he will do so again. In two weeks from Saturday we will pack our small sets of possessions and take the main road west. We could take a boat up the river to Parramatta but that's expensive for all of us, so let's make sure our shoes are patched and that we only take what we really need. Start saying goodbye to your friends and let your employers know so they can plan your replacements.

"I know I am asking a lot of you all. Thomas and Patrick, you are old enough at twenty-one to make your own decisions and we will understand if you want to stay behind."

Thomas interrupted quickly before his father could continue. "Father, there is little here for us, and Patrick and I have talked about staying versus moving on and had already decided if you asked we would go west with everyone. We've heard versions of those stories ourselves and frankly are looking forward to seeing what we might find. We're all strong, and others less able than us have clearly made the trek, so we all can do it too. I want to see the Blue Mountains and wonder how close we might get. For some reason I find them totally fascinating. Perhaps because they are the new frontier here and there was nothing so daunting back home."

All at once everyone was talking and anticipating the trip to come. Both parents were pleasantly surprised and afterwards expressed their relief to one another at the solidarity of their family. Ellen observed: "Maybe we don't give our children enough credit, Matthew. I guess the two sets of twins are essentially adults and totally capable of forming their own opinions and outlooks. Perhaps we should seek their advice more often."

"As usual, you are more perceptive than me, dear wife. They certainly still are a joy to my heart. All of them. One day they'll leave us. I hope I'll be ready when that happens."

Several years after the route across the mountains had been forged in 1813, Governor Macquarie urged the construction of a road from Sydney to Penrith. Sixteen sandstone markers indicated the mileage to both towns and these became the guidelines for the Burkes' progress west. In the early days of its existence the road was a major symbol of progress. Its point of departure was George Street and Sydney Cove, the genesis of the colony. Its route went west to Parramatta. Beyond, its symbolic character became more apparent, as the topography of long parallel ridges dipping down to the Nepean in prelude to the ascent of the great ramparts of the Blue Mountains on the other side of the river began to unfold. The road held a strange sense of promise to its travellers, a sense of anticipation quite unlike that felt on any other road out of Sydney.

And so it was for Matthew and Ellen Burke and their children. Ahead lay hope for the new life they desperately sought. The children took delight in counting off the miles. Every bullock team coming towards them stopped and they exchanged greetings. Matthew asked about work, Ellen asked about housing and food supplies. And that's how they learned about Regentville.

The first view of the estate took their breath away. In the distance as they approached they could see an enormous mansion as the nucleus in a cluster of ancillary buildings of immense variety. The sun shone on the front pillars of the two-storey house and on some of the outbuildings. They had seen nothing comparable in their travels west, and the only edifice that came into mind was Government House back in Sydney. The structure was magnificent and the family was awed as their eyes swept back and forth.

"How can this be?" exclaimed Elizabeth. "It is so far from Sydney, and in the middle of nowhere. Are we sure this is not also a giant inn, rather than a house for a nobleman? Who could need all that space?"

"And what on earth are all those buildings, I wonder?" chimed in Ann. "The smoke from the chimney at right suggests that may be a kitchen, but could the next two be quarters for servants? They look like small houses with their windows. My, oh my. Are you sure this is the place, Father?"

"Look," cried Ellen. "That smaller building must be a laundry of some sort, for there goes a maid with a basket of clothes to hang on a line somewhere, I warrant. She even wears a uniform. My heavens, it's a very rich man who lives here for sure."

The men had wandered a little ahead and stood open-mouthed as they observed vast sheep paddocks, and grapevines and vegetable plots stretching between the road and the river in the distance. In shock, and now with a little trepidation, wondering if they were about to step way out of class, they all trudged up the main drive to the circular garden with its fountain splashing happily and small birds bathing in its waters. A broad-shouldered man with thick forearms sitting in a rocker on the front veranda rose as they approached.

"We met Mr. Thomas Jamison along the road and he suggested we stop by," Matthew said. "We're looking for jobs."

"He was probably on his way to Sydney," the man said. "I'm George and I run the butchery here. How can I help you? Have you come far? You look thirsty. Let me arrange some lemonade."

With that he went inside and came back a couple of minutes later to find the Burkes sitting in the shade against the wall of the house out of the direct sun. Matthew jumped up and introduced himself. "I'm Matthew Burke, from Donegal County, Ireland, and this is my family. We met the manager three days ago on the road to Penrith. He invited us here to work alongside the convicts."

"Did he now? If that's the case we must look after you properly. I'll arrange to have some fresh bread and butter provided as well. Do rest up."

Little did any of them know how much George was enjoying himself. Ten years ago he had arrived at the estate accompanied by a guard from the Sydney garrison. He vividly recalled how he had been treated on arrival. Not as a convict, but as a man with skills to be used on the estate. He had been called 'sir,' and a pretty maid had asked him to wait 'please' as the manager had been called away temporarily. He hadn't been treated so deferentially in years. Once again, as with previous strangers, he could reciprocate, and he treasured the opportunity.

A maid dressed in black with a white apron on and a white band in her hair carried out a tray with ten glasses, a number of little lace doilies, and a giant pitcher of lemonade. She set it down on the small serving table and George invited the Burkes to help themselves. Too nervous to speak up, the children mumbled grateful thanks and savored the soothing drink. Baby David gurgled and Ellen raised him to her breast.

"So tell me your story," George requested. "I'm all ears."

In 1842 Sir John had had built on his property a four-storied woollen mill for the manufacture of tweed. It seemed like a logical investment that saved the transport costs of wool sent to England and the reverse costs of shipping finished clothes, blankets, drapes, and rugs back to Australia. He imported not only the necessary machinery but the operatives for the mill as well—carders, weavers, dyers, etc., along with their families. For a long time the mill was the scene of a busy industry and represented one of the first major industrial pastoral innovations in the colony of which there were not enough to achieve balance against the need for unskilled labour. For so many years this building that was welcome landmark on the landscape to those traveling east down the mountains heading to the Nepean.

It wasn't hard to accommodate some of the Burke females into the mill's workforce, and the males into helping manage the livestock as Sir John had recently acquired a large run at Kyogle on the Richmond River, called Richmond Head, and had sent some of the local Regentville hands there to organize its function. Timing worked to everyone's benefit. The Burkes were fortunate to find work for so many in their family, because elsewhere the depression still held sway, although the political economy struggled on.

About the time the Burkes had been preparing to leave Drumcairn, Sir John's second daughter, Jane Rebecca, was getting married. The lucky man was Captain William Russell of His Majesty's 28th Regiment. At age sixteen, Jane was married by Special Licence in Penrith on 11 Mar 1841. Her father, in his generosity, gave the couple a patch of land within Simeon Lord's original nearby grant which Sir John had purchased, and they built a home there. Sir John had a lot of confidence in Captain Russell, having him manage some of the wider family costs. Over the years Jane produced eleven children, John Jamison in 1842, William Fred in 1843, and the others, Jane Augusta Matilda, Fred Berkeley, Amy Charlotte Isabelle, Arthur Hamilton Trevellyn, Reginald Lionel de Courcy, Florence Mary Emily, Sydney Staven Septimus, Charles Wesley Trewlaney and Wentworth Charles William Octavos, up until 1860.

On 4 June 1842, Sir John's third daughter, Mary Elizabeth, married Frederick Browne Russell, William's brother, also of the 28th Regiment. The marriage took place under Special Licence at St. Philip's church in Sydney. Mary was three months shy of her sixteenth birthday at the time. It's possible that both girls married early in light of the slowing economy, looking to their own security, or possibly even with the advice of their father anticipating future economic issues.

In November 1842 John Hosking was elected the first mayor of Sydney. The mayor's firm of Hughes & Hosking became insolvent in 1843, marking the depth of the depression, and bringing down with it the Bank of Australia, to which the two principals, who had borrowed extensively, owed more than £155,000. Hosking was forced to retire from the corporation.

There were six major banks in Sydney at the time. Other banks also failed, including the Port Philip Bank and the Sydney Banking Company. None escaped the monetary crisis and the widespread sea of concern over financial stability. The Bank of New South Wales left 1,356 Sydney residents insolvent. The New South Wales financial system lacked a lender of last resort (such as the Bank of England), which contributed to a significant contraction of the money supply aggravating the crisis. Two important monetary recovery measures directly concerned with repairing liquidity during the crisis were approved: a) the Monetary Confidence Bill of 1843 seeking to create a government note issue of £200,000 secured by land, and b) the *Lien on Wool and Stock Mortgage Act (NSW) 1843* seeking to increase the money supply through renewed bank lending on the basis of more effective security rights over wool and stock.

These initiatives plus others helped turn things around, but it was too late for Sir John. As a founding father and the Bank of New South Wales' second biggest stockholder, he was seriously affected personally by the liquidity issue, and narrowly escaped bankruptcy.

His days of great wealth had come to an end.

18. The Power and the Glory....

Plans that had been set in motion pre–bank failure were still financed at the estate including construction of a building of family quarters for the field employees. But nothing new was undertaken. The strain and stress of complex financial arrangements, both bank and personal, caused Sir John's health to decline. No longer was he the gay, effervescent, charismatic leader that once strode the halls of the house or rode out into the pastures to inspect the new lambs or watch his horses being exercised. For one of the first times in his life he felt guilty for letting down his fellow man, and for his inability to repair the damage done.

A pall fell over the house and estate and affected everyone from the youngest child to the long-time farm hands like George Dent, who had received his ticket of leave while working for his host for over eleven years. With his health deteriorating, and the need to provide financial security to those important to him, Sir John married Mary Griffiths on Thursday 8 February 1844 at St. Philip's Church of England in Sydney. Archdeacon William Cowper performed the ceremony.

After twenty years as Sir John's housekeeper and mistress, the mother of six of his children suddenly become Dame Mary Jamison. A just reward.

St. Philip's Church of England had served the Jamison family several times. The original church had been built in 1793 at Church Hill instigating the oldest Anglican Church parish in Australia. Five years later convicts burned down the wattle and daub constructed building, but it was replaced in 1810 with a stone church, characterised by a one-hundred-fifty-foot-high round clock tower.

As 1844 wore on, Sir John became weaker and weaker. Estate employees viewed Sir John as a charismatic, innovative, socially conscious leader. That his presence, his reign, his charm, and warm-heartedness might be in jeopardy was hard to contemplate. He was an institution, their savant, leader, and employer. Without him their world would crumble, be ill defined, and almost unimaginable. There was sadness everywhere as the realisation set in that the great man's life was coming to an end. After years of semi-hedonistic, fast-paced living, coupled with endless days of personal property management and tireless commitment to the advancement of the country, his body screamed for relief. No longer could it keep up with the demands he had made of it over time. He was, after all, sixty-eight years old, and deserved to slow down.

But it was too late. On 29 June this flamboyant Irishman finally succumbed to the call from his God, passing away at his elegant home by the banks of the Nepean.

The whole estate was grief-stricken. Fast riders were sent in all directions to his various properties bearing the startling news. The governor of the state was notably distressed, as were many dignitaries and explorers who had spent time enjoying Sir John's hospitality at Regentville. Two days after death, in a simple ceremony, Sir John was buried in an above-ground tomb in the graveyard of St. Stephen The Martyr Anglican Church in Penrith. The church and cemetery had been consecrated on 16 July 1839, and it was their very existence that allowed the village of Penrith to be later designated as a town. The inscription on the tomb read

In Memory of
SIR JOHN JAMISON M.D.R.N.
PHYSICIAN TO THE BALTIC FLEET 1807
H.M.S.GORGON
DIED AT REGENTVILLE 29th JUNE 1844

Mourners paid their respects as high society men held hats against their chests, and women wore veils across their faces. Tears were evident in many eyes. The mourning at Regentville continued for days, as the loss of the man left everyone wondering what his departure would mean—for his family, for the estate, and for themselves. No quick answers were to be forthcoming.

For the moment Mary was in charge, her first priority being to get the family papers and finances in order. Out of the ether came both legitimate and spurious claims against the estate, many producing unpaid bills and demands for restitution. Son Robert, who later was to become a member of the Legislative Assembly of New South Wales from 1856 to 1860, was her biggest help at the tender age of fifteen. It was not the most pleasant of times, with bickering throughout the extended family about what to do with the estate, and some resentment that Mary had inherited so much at such a late date.

One prime example illustrates the tension that existed. On Monday 24 February 1845, the Supreme Court considered the case of Bradley vs Jamison. The *Sydney Morning Herald* reported:

> In this case, James Bradley, late of Parramatta, and now of Kissing Point, schoolmaster, was plaintiff, and Jane Mary Jamison, executrix of the late Sir John Jamison, was defendant.
>
> Counsel for the Plaintiff, Mr. Windeyer; for the defence, Mr. Darvall.
>
> The plaintiff claimed £36 3s. 6d., being three quarters' board and education at £10 per quarter, and the balance for extras supplied to one Thomas Jamison or Cains, a reputed son of the late Sir John Jamison. The defendant had paid £12 10s. into Court in full of all claims.
>
> For the plaintiff, it was proved that Thomas Jamison or Cains had been placed in his charge by Sir John Jamison, in 1837, and that from that time to the period from which he now claimed, payment had been made by Sir John Jamison or his agents.
>
> The defence was, that as early as November 1843, notice had been given to the plaintiff by Lieutenant William Russell, then acting as agent for Sir John Jamison, that no further payments would be made, and further, that Sir John Jamison died in June, 1844, and therefore no such claim as sought to be established, up to 6th January, 1845, could exist.
>
> A subsequent payment, however, to this alleged notice, was shown to have been made by Dr. Dobie, who was appointed attorney for Sir John Jamison in place of Lieutenant William Russell.
>
> The Jury found a verdict for the full amount claimed, deducting the £12 10s paid into Court, and 1s. damages.
>
> His Honor certified for costs.

Work continued unabated at the estate. Cattle, sheep, and poultry still needed management, as did the crops, the orchards, and the vineyard. The horses needed exercise, and the irrigation system, the laundry, and other mechanical facets needed engineering maintenance. At the house, food still needed to be prepared and young children taught their lessons. Workers were happy to still have their jobs, although concerned at how long their employment might continue. One of the more jubilant occasions was the marriage of the popular butcher, George Dent, to one of the woollen mill girls, Ann Burke, in April 1845, although they left shortly after when George opened his own butcher's shop in High Street, Penrith.

1846 passed into 1847 and in December came the not-unexpected news that Regentville was to be sold.

A portion of the splendid estate of Regentville, consisting of 1560 acres, about 600 of which are cleared and stumped, and about 150 under cultivation. Together with the elegant family mansion house, garden, grounds, vineyards, etc. To be sold by auction by Mr. Lyons at his mart on Tuesday the 21st December....... The following valuable improvements have been made on the Hawkestone Grant; first, "Regentville House", substantially built of stone with a tasteful Colonnade in front and on each side, surmounted with an Iron Balcony from which there is a delightful prospect of the adjacent country. It contains an Entrance Hall and 15 rooms, viz; 2 drawing rooms, 1 dining room, 1 breakfast room, 1 study, 1 library and cabinet, 9 bedrooms, the principal staircase is also stone built and circular. A wash-house and laundry are attached, and there are spacious cellars under the house. The right wing consists of an immense coach-house with store above; the left wing contains the billiard room. The out offices are also stone built, and consist of 2 kitchens and a bakehouse communicating with the house by a covered way, a servants' hall and 7 bedrooms adjoining; the whole being under one roof. All the above offices are contained within an area of 180 feet square, enclosed by a substantial stone wall about 10 feet high. In the rear of the foregoing, adjoining the wall, are the handsome stone stables, which consists of one 10-stall and one 4-stall, with three large boxes and two harness rooms. The lofts are over the whole of the above stabling, and are about 160 feet in length by 15 feet breadth. the stable yard is enclosed by a paling, and contains also 3 loose boxes, slab-built, with loft over them. Adjoining the stable yard at the back lies the Garden, covering about 4 acres, full of choice fruit trees, vegetables, etc., and contains the gardener's house. In the rear of the garden, a shed is partitioned off, and railed in to accommodate about thirty colts; it is well secured by a substantial fence, and has a paddock attached with contains stockyards and draughting yards. The Vineyard is on the left of the house, and contains about 7 acres of terraced vines, and 3 1/2 acres of field vineyard. It also has a stone built house, containing four rooms, a large cellar for manufacturing wine, with wine press and still. Immediately in front of the wine cellar there is a large dam, receiving the water from two gullies: is about 300 feet in circumference, by about 10 feet in depth, and has never been dry.

It was a sad time for all those who had been associated with the estate over the years as it was subdivided and parcels sold off while the mansion and surrounds were converted into a hotel. Regentville had been an influential part of many convicts' and free settlers' lives. Now the sanctuary it once was for them, along with its magnificence, style, and vitality, was gone.

Few convicts probably had it as good as those who served at Regentville. Not only was Sir John Jamison a well-respected master, the whole environment was incredibly unique. A giant house essentially in the middle of nowhere, built like a fine English mansion. Only Government houses built for crown appointees offered any sense of similarity in style and purpose. And no convicts served in those, as they represented the values of members of the peak of the upper classes of English society. Completely at the opposite end of the social spectrum to the "wretched, immoral, and depraved" criminals they were sent to guard and reform.

For Sir John's employed convicts, authoritarian rule was almost non-existent. In general, those assigned to Regentville had no wish to hurry and leave, except those who missed cobblestone streets, brick houses, a plethora of pubs, the noise of trains and coaches, and nearby churches and shops, and crowds. For those folks, even though there was a beautiful river at hand, it had no wharves or warehouses or grand sailing ships, as did the mighty Thames. In a different vein for others, even the beauty of the unusual birds and the kangaroos and the possums couldn't overcome the existence of snakes and bushrangers and strange insects. When they could, convicts so affected applied to work for a different master in Sydney or Parramatta. Their experience at Regentville usually stood them in good stead and it was a rare circumstance when Sir John did not put in a good recommendation for them.

The conversion of the mansion at Regentville to a hotel was a notion that was unfathomable to most, and many were happy to leave the area and not have to see the desecration that would befall their home. As upsetting as that was, another great sadness was the potential loss of friendships that had developed and been nurtured over time, some covering a decade or more.

The Dent family was one of the few that stayed in the area, increasing to six children along the way. The eldest son, William, born in 1846, developed a smart business sense, acquiring land, as well as managing the butcher business after both his parents died. He watched the Regentville mansion go through many phases—from the initial hotel to a mental 'lunatic asylum' in 1856 to 1863, the home for the new tweed mill owner, back to a private hotel leased by the Shiels family and called The Abels Family Hotel. On 22 May, 1869 the house was destroyed by fire. The _Sydney Morning Herald_ of 27 May tells of the inquest into the fire where the jury concluded that "the house was wilfully and maliciously set on fire by some person or persons unknown." The mill ceased work and the big building, though still standing high, became a picturesque ruin.

By 1881-82 William Dent owned the butcher shop and a house attached, plus the slaughter yards in Mulgoa Road. Another lot he acquired included the ruins of the burnt-out Regentville mansion. William removed sandstone blocks from the remains of the structure and used them to build Ormonde House in High Street, Penrith. An extract from _Personal Reminiscences of Ernest William Orth, 1872-1958_, provided by Penrith City Library, states: 'A gentleman named Dent demolished Sir John's residence, and on removing a rafter during the work, discovered a cavity in which was deposited a pickle bottle full of gold and silver coins. Mr. Dent never disclosed the sum the bottle contained.' William operated Ormonde House as a boarding house with resident manager.

As a final indignity for Regentville, some of its stone blocks were used to form gutters in parts of Station Street and Belmore Street in Penrith. Equally ungracious was the placement of the stained glass window from Sir John's private chapel into a public hotel. It carried the words from David's song in Psalm 122: "I was glad when they said unto me, let us go into the house of the Lord."

Over twenty years, hundreds of men and women, from indigenous natives, to lowly convicts, to dignified aristocrats, had entered the house of Sir John. None had left without learning something from the great man. He had served England, Norway, and Australia in various capacities over his lifetime.

It was his adopted country, Australia, which benefitted most.

Author's Biography

Warren's great great grandfather was an English convict; his wife an Irish free settler. They met in 1843 on Sir John Jamison's vast estate, named Regentville, located 35 miles from Sydney on the banks of the Nepean River. The property encompassed over 11,000 acres, and ran cattle, sheep, and pigs alongside major grain fields, vineyards, as well as irrigated orchards. A magnificent mansion housed the Jamison family and became the retreat of governors and other prominent citizens.

Warren has extensively researched the history of Australia during convict times, writing about the pioneers, citizens, and criminals who forged a new society in an unknown land. Sir John was a unique individual who helped create a culture that provided a life far better than would have been available to many back in England and Ireland.

One of Warren's goals is to make sure the efforts of such pioneers, their beliefs, and their dedication in forging a new country, are not forgotten. His colonial times stories are known for their seamless integration of true historical events. In this instance he's particularly grateful to Sir John for providing the place where his ancestors met.

Warren was raised in Sydney, attended ANU and the University of Adelaide, before getting a Ph.D. at the University of Minnesota. He taught in the USA for many years, before entering the private sector, where he worked at Eli Lilly, American Airlines, and Microsoft creating new businesses and applying information systems to strategic market applications. With numerous academic publications to his credit, and hundreds of business presentations behind him, he has recently turned his writing talents to more personal endeavours.

Index

www.ingramcontent.com/pod-product-compliance
Lightning Source LLC
Chambersburg PA
CBHW052041090426
42739CB00010B/1994